ROUGH GUIDES **WITHDRAWN**

POCKET **ROUGH GUIDE**
BRUGES & GHENT

WRITTEN AND RESEARCHED BY
PHIL LEE

CONTENTS

BRUGES & GHENT

Passing through Bruges in 1820, William Wordsworth declared that this was where he discovered "a deeper peace than in deserts found". Indeed, Wordsworth was one of the first Victorians to fall in love with a city, whose charms continue to enthral its many visitors: Bruges's slender canals are flanked by an enchanting ensemble of ancient buildings, punctuated with a string of excellent museums, principally the Groeninge Museum with its world-class collection of early Flemish paintings. Neighbouring Ghent boasts its share of handsome medieval buildings too, and also possesses one of the artistic wonders of the medieval world: the *Adoration of the Mystic Lamb* altarpiece by Jan van Eyck. Nonetheless, the atmosphere here is markedly different from that in Bruges: the tourist industry supplements but does not dominate the local economy and Ghent is first and foremost a vibrant Flemish city.

Ghent's beautiful old town

For the modern palate, Bruges's blend of antique architectural styles, from tiny brick cottages to gracious Classical mansions, is a welcome relief and retreat. It certainly brings out the romance in many of its visitors – stay here long enough and you can't help but be amazed by the number of couples wandering its canals hand-in-hand, cheek-to-cheek. Neither does it matter much that a large part of Bruges is not quite what it seems: many buildings have been carefully constructed to resemble their medieval predecessors. Bruges has spent time and money preserving its image, rendering almost everything that's new in various versions of medieval style, and the result is one of Europe's most beautiful city centres. Ghent, on the other hand, is a vital, bustling metropolis whose booming restaurant and bar scene wends its way across a charming cityscape, comprising a network of narrow canals overseen by dozens of antique red-brick houses. If Bruges is a tourist industry with a town attached, Ghent is the reverse – a proudly Flemish city which, with a population of around 250,000, is now Belgium's third-largest conurbation.

Bruges and Ghent share a similar history. Both prospered as lynchpins of the cloth trade,

A guild house in Ghent

turning high-quality English wool into clothing that was exported all over the world. It was an immensely profitable business and one that made Bruges, in particular, a focus of international trade. Through the city's harbours, Flemish cloth was exchanged for hogs from Denmark, spices from Venice, hides from Ireland, wax from Russia and furs from Bulgaria. However, despite (or perhaps because of) this lucrative state of affairs, Bruges and Ghent were dogged by war. The weavers and merchants of both cities were

When to visit

Bruges and Ghent are all-year destinations. Both cities enjoy a fairly standard temperate climate, with warm, if mild, summers and cold winters, without much snow. The warmest months are usually June, July and August (averaging 18°C); the coldest, December and January (averaging 2°C), when short daylight hours and weak sunlight can make the weather seem colder (and wetter) than it actually is. Rain is always a possibility, even in summer, which actually has more rainfall than either autumn or winter. Warm days in April, May and early June, when the light has the clarity of springtime, are especially appealing, especially in Bruges, before the tourists of summertime arrive in full force. If you're planning a short visit, it's worth noting that many of the cities' museums are closed on Mondays.

What's new

In the past few years, Ghent has emerged as a gastronomic pace setter, witnessing the opening of a string of inventive, much-vaunted restaurants – Roots (see page 116), De Lieve (see page 115) and Chambre Séparée (see page 126) are three cases in point. Bruges trades on its continuity, but the city's main concert hall, the Concertgebouw (see page 147), has made sterling efforts to open itself to casual visitors and now offers an enjoyable programme of guided tours.

dependent on the goodwill of the kings of England for their wool supply, but their feudal overlords, the counts of Flanders and their successors the dukes of Burgundy, were vassals of the rival king of France. Consequently, whenever France and England were at war – which was often – both cities found themselves in a precarious position.

The Habsburgs swallowed Flanders – including Bruges and Ghent –into their empire in 1482, and the sour relations that existed with the new rulers led to the decline of the two cities. Economically and politically marooned, Bruges was especially hard hit and simply withered away, its houses deserted, its canals empty and its money spirited away by the departing merchants. Some four centuries later, Georges Rodenbach's novel *Bruges-la-Morte* alerted well-heeled Europeans to the town's aged, quiet charms, and Bruges attracted its first wave of tourists. Many of them – especially the British – settled here and came to play a leading role in preserving the city's architectural heritage. Ghent, meanwhile, fared rather better, struggling on as a minor port and trading depot until its fortunes were revived by the development of a cotton spinning industry in the early nineteenth century. Within the space of forty years, Ghent was jam-packed with factories producing all manner of industrial goods and, although the city has moved on from its industrial base, it remains economically buoyant and is Belgium's third-largest metropolis with a population of around 250,000.

The Concertgebouw, the main concert hall in Bruges

Where to...

Shop

The holy trinity of Belgian shopping is chocolates, beer and lace. There is no shortage of chocolate and beer shops – both chain and family-run – in Bruges and Ghent, but lace is rather different. In Bruges, lace is sold in shops all around the city, but most of it is only imported, machine-made pieces – the only real exception is 't Apostelientje. In Ghent there isn't much evidence of lace at all. If you're after international chain stores, you'll find plenty of outlets, especially in Ghent. Most are on the three main shopping streets: **Langemunt** and **Veldstraat** in Ghent and **Noordzandstraat** in Bruges.
OUR FAVOURITES: Bruges: Reisboekhandel see page 34; The Chocolate Line see page 65; 't Apostelientje see page 86. Ghent: Tierenteyn see page 113; Van Hecke see page 113; De Hopduvel see page 126.

Eat

As you might expect of a major tourist destination, Bruges has many restaurants, but a large number of them are aimed at outsiders, so standards are often patchy, especially around the Markt. That said, the city does possess a good supply of first-rate places to eat. Ghent's restaurant scene is arguably more reliable and indeed the city has an enviable reputation for its pace-setting restaurants. They range from Michelin-starred places with an international menu to more local haunts, which characteristically offer traditional Flemish cuisine with a twist.
OUR FAVOURITES: Bruges: De Schaar see page 68; Pomperlut see page 68. Ghent: Maison Elza see page 115; De Lieve see page 115.

Drink

With every justification, Belgium is famous for its beers and its bars – and Bruges and Ghent are no exception. In both cities, the hallmark bars are small and dark affairs. Almost all the best bars have beer menus, with some running to several hundred brews, mostly bottled, but a few on tap. Many bars also sell jenever, which is similar to gin, made from grain spirit and flavoured with juniper berries. There are two main types – the young (*jonge*) and the smoother old (*oude*), but both are served ice cold in shot glasses. In both cities, the best bars are dotted around the city centre and the vast majority are within easy walking distance of each other.
OUR FAVOURITES: Bruges: De Garre see page 45; L'Estaminet see page 69. Ghent: 't Dreupelkot see page 116; Dulle Griet see page 116.

Go out

Frankly, you don't visit Bruges for its nightlife, though the city's festivals and special events (see page 146) do provide a boost to what is a fairly modest scene: Bruges has just two really good late-night places, one with live music, the other with DJ sounds. In Ghent, the most boisterous part of the city is the student quarter on and around Overpoortstraat, where there are a lot of heaving late-night bars and clubs.
OUR FAVOURITES: Bruges: B-in see page 69; Est Wijnbar see page 45. Ghent: Vooruit see page 127; Decadence see page 127.

Bruges at a glance

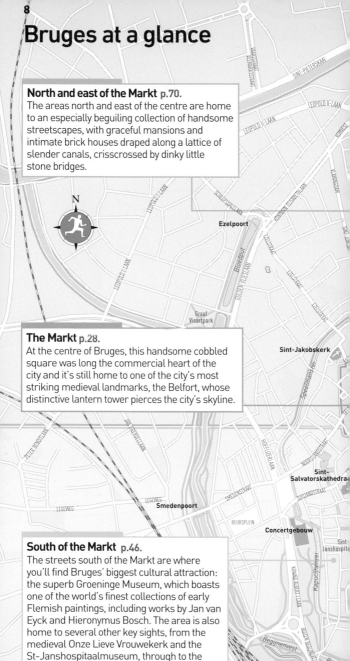

North and east of the Markt p.70.

The areas north and east of the centre are home to an especially beguiling collection of handsome streetscapes, with graceful mansions and intimate brick houses draped along a lattice of slender canals, crisscrossed by dinky little stone bridges.

The Markt p.28.

At the centre of Bruges, this handsome cobbled square was long the commercial heart of the city and it's still home to one of the city's most striking medieval landmarks, the Belfort, whose distinctive lantern tower pierces the city's skyline.

South of the Markt p.46.

The streets south of the Markt are where you'll find Bruges' biggest cultural attraction: the superb Groeninge Museum, which boasts one of the world's finest collections of early Flemish paintings, including works by Jan van Eyck and Hieronymus Bosch. The area is also home to several other key sights, from the medieval Onze Lieve Vrouwekerk and the St-Janshospitaalmuseum, through to the whitewashed cottages of the Begijnhof and the Minnewater, the so-called "Lake of Love".

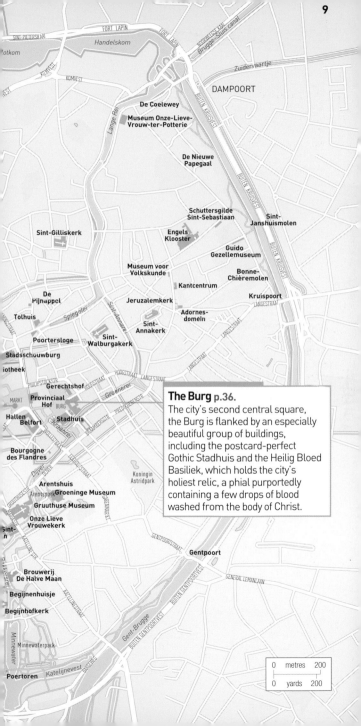

The Burg p.36.

The city's second central square, the Burg is flanked by an especially beautiful group of buildings, including the postcard-perfect Gothic Stadhuis and the Heilig Bloed Basiliek, which holds the city's holiest relic, a phial purportedly containing a few drops of blood washed from the body of Christ.

| 0 | metres | 200 |
| 0 | yards | 200 |

Ghent at a glance

Central Ghent p.94.

Ghent's ancient centre holds a glorious set of Gothic buildings, including the stirring St-Baafskathedraal (also home to the remarkable Adoration of the Mystic Lamb by Jan van Eyck), St Niklaaskerk, the medieval guild houses of the Graslei, and a forbidding castle, Het Gravensteen.

Het Gravensteen

REKELINGESTRAAT

Oude Vismijn

Leie

Design Museum

Groot Vleeshuis

Sint-Niklaaskerk

Sint-Michielskerk

Het Pand

Museum Arnold Vander Haeghen

Hôtel d'Han Steenhuys

PAPEGAAISTRAAT

ANNONCIADENSTR.

GEBR. VANDEVELDESTR.

ZONNESTRAAT

BERNARD SPAELAAN

Concert Handelst

Gerechtshof

Opera Ghent

NEDERKOUTER

MARTELAARSLAAN

MARTELAARSLAAN

MARTELAARSLAAN

Coupure

Leie

GROOT-BRITTANNIËLAAN

ROGGHÜLLENLAAN

De Bijloke

STAM

KORTRIJKSEPOORTSTRAAT

Damme p.88.

A popular day-trip from Bruges, the pretty little village of Damme perches beside a canal 7km to the northeast of the city; it's best reached by bicycle.

IJZERLAAN

CHARLES DE KERCHOVELAAN

Citadelpark

S.M.A.K. (Stedelijk Museum voor Actuele Kunst)

Damme

Bruges

0   miles   8

0   kilometres   10

Ghent

STEENDAM

STEENDAM

Sint-Jacobskerk

DAMPOORTSTRAAT

RODETORENK AAI

HAGELANDKAAI

DIJK-ZUID

OKTROOIPLEIN

KASTEELLAAN

Sint-Baafsabdij

Leie

dhuis

Stadshal
Lakenhalle

ort

Sint-Baafskathedraal

Geeraard de
Duivelsteen

KUIPERSKAAI

VLAANDERENSTRAAT

SINT-JACOBSNIEUWSTRAAT

BRABANTDAM

MARK \

KEIZER KARELSTRAAT

KEIZER KARELSTRAAT

Coyendanspark

BRABANTDAM

VLAANDERENSTRAAT

ZUIDSTATIONSTRAAT

SINT-ANNA

LANGE VIOLETTESTRAAT

NIEUWBOSSTR.

KASTEELLAAN

KASTEELLAAN

Vooruit

FRANKLIN ROOSEVELTLAAN

GRAAF VAN VLAANDERENPLEIN

ZUIDPARKLAAN

LANGE VIOLETTESTRAAT

BRUSSELSEPOORTSTRAAT

FRANKLIN ROOSEVELTLAAN

Koning
Albertpark

Sint-
Pietersabdij

Muinkpark

Kunsthal

Southern and eastern Ghent p.118.
Ghent's two leading fine art museums –
historic works at MSK and contemporary
art at S.M.A.K. – are located a couple of
kilometres south of the centre, not far
from the main train station.

MSK
(Museum voor
Shone Kunsten)

CITADELLAAN

| 0 | metres | 200 |
| 0 | yards | 200 |

15

Things not to miss

It's not really possible to see everything that Bruges and Ghent have to offer in one trip – and we don't suggest you try. What follows is a selective taste of their highlights – from eye-catching architecture to exquisite art.

< Onze Lieve Vrouwekerk, Bruges
See page 54
This intriguing medieval church is home to a Michelangelo *Madonna* and two superbly crafted medieval sarcophagi in the choir.

> St-Walburgakerk, Bruges
See page 75
Of all the parish churches in Bruges, this fluent Baroque extravagance, built for the Jesuits in the seventeenth century, is perhaps the most charming.

∨ Het Gravensteen, Ghent
See page 104
Ghent's stern and forbidding castle, Het Gravensteen, has long cast a steely eye over the city centre.

< **Adoration of the Mystic Lamb, Ghent**
See page 110
Displayed in Ghent's St-Baafskathedraal, Jan van Eyck's visionary painting celebrates the Lamb of God, the symbol of Christ's sacrifice.

> **Kantcentrum, Bruges**
See page 78
The Kantcentrum (lace centre) exhibits a small but exquisite collection of antique lace and hosts informal demonstrations of traditional lace-making.

< **Minnewater, Bruges**
See page 64
The so-called "Lake of Love" is reckoned to be one of the city's most romantic spots – and it certainly attracts the canoodlers.

∨ **S.M.A.K., Ghent**
See page 119
Ghent's premier art gallery has an excellent collection of Belgian art, from the Flemish Primitives through to Magritte.

∧ **Chocolate Line, Bruges**
See page 65
Most chocolate shops in
Bruges are chains, but this one
isn't – and the chocolates are
mouthwateringly divine.

< **St-Baafskathedraal, Ghent**
See page 94
At the heart of Ghent,
St-Baafskathedraal is
one of Belgium's finest
and most distinguished
Gothic churches.

∧ **The Belfort, Bruges**

See page 31

One of Belgium's most distinctive landmarks, the soaring lantern tower of the Belfort (belfry) pierces the skyline of central Bruges.

∨ **Groeninge Museum, Bruges**

See page 50

The leading art museum in Bruges, internationally famous for its wonderful collection of early Flemish paintings, from van Eyck onwards.

∧ St-Janshospitaal, Bruges
See page 56
This former medieval hospital is now a museum housing a delightful sample of the paintings of Hans Memling.

< Design Museum, Ghent
See page 103
With its charming sequence of period rooms at the front and contemporary design at the back, this is one of Ghent's most enjoyable museums.

< **St-Baafsabdij, Ghent**
See page 124
Off the beaten track, the rambling
ruins of this charming, mostly
medieval abbey are well worth
the detour.

∨ **Heilig Bloed Basiliek,
Bruges**
See page 36
The city's most important shrine,
home to the much-venerated
phial of the Holy Blood, its
contents reputedly washed from
the body of the crucified Christ.

Day One in Bruges

The Burg. See page 36. Begin in the heart of Bruges. Few squares in Europe can match the architectural delights of the Burg, home to both the Stadhuis and the Heilig Bloed Basiliek (Basilica of the Holy Blood), one of the holiest shrines of medieval Christendom.

Rozenhoedkaai. See page 34. Bruges is remarkably picturesque, but make sure you check the view back towards the Belfort from the Rozenhoedkaai (the Quay of the Rosary), as it's extraordinarily beautiful.

The Markt. See page 28. The Markt is a charming central square, its cobblestones shadowed by the Belfort (belfry). If you have the energy, climb its distinctive lantern tower for views across the city.

Heilig Bloed Basiliek

Lunch. See page 34. Of all the cafés near the Markt, *L.b DbB* is the pick. It's a neat little place serving absolutely delicious salads at competitive prices.

Groeninge Museum. See page 50. Allow at least a couple of hours to explore the city's premier fine-art gallery and brush up on your knowledge of early Flemish art from the likes of Gerard David and Jan van Eyck.

Onze Lieve Vrouwekerk. See page 54. Few would say this historic church is pretty, but it is fascinating – from its grave frescoes and Renaissance mausoleums through to its delicately carved Michelangelo sculpture.

View from the Rozenhoedkaai

Dinner. See page 68. Escape the more crowded s of the city and stroll out to *De r*, an infinitely cosy, canalside nt.

page 69. Later, drop et to sample those beers.

Groeninge Museum

Day Two in Bruges

St-Janshospitaalmuseum. See page 57. One of the most talented of the early Flemish painters was Hans Memling and this museum holds an exquisite selection of his work.

St-Salvatorskathedraal. See page 57. This is the most important church in Bruges and home to a set of tapestries and the matching paintings from which they were copied – a rarity indeed.

🍴 **Lunch**. See page 86. Take a break in style at *Blackbird*, an agreeable café with a menu that's strong on all things healthy.

A painting in St-Salvatorskathedraal

Spiegelrei canal. See page 74. Stroll the easy sweep of one of the most graceful canals in Bruges, its blue-black waters flanked by handsome old mansions redolent of Bruges' late-medieval heyday.

St-Walburgakerk. See page 75. The very Catholic citizens of Bruges have punctuated their city with lovely churches. This is one of the most striking with its flowing Baroque facade.

The Adornesdomein. See page 77. Learn about the rollercoaster life and times of one of Bruges' most important medieval families and check out their unusual church, the Jeruzalemkerk.

The Spiegelrei canal

Kantcentrum. See page 78. Admire the intricate lacework of the women of Bruges, hundreds of whom were once employed in this key industry.

🍴 **Dinner**. See page 86. Dine at the excellent *Bistro Pro Deo* in a 16th-century townhouse on Langestraat. Traditional food with a soul-music soundtrack.

Drink. See page 87. Continue to *Café Vlissinghe*, one of the oldest bars in Bruges. Try the traditional Flemish bar snacks.

An exhibition at the Ador

Day One in Ghent

St-Baafskathedraal. See page 94. The obvious place to start an exploration of Ghent is the cathedral, home to the city's greatest artistic treasure: the *Adoration of the Mystic Lamb*.

St-Niklaaskerk. See page 99. Admire the peaked roofs, arching buttresses and pencil-thin turrets of St-Niklaaskerk – the most visually arresting of all Ghent's churches.

The Graslei. See page 102. Head for Tussen Bruggen, which was once the main harbour, and work your way along the decorated series of medieval guild houses.

Design Museum. See page 103. A hymn of praise to Belgian decorative and applied arts, this fascinating museum displays period rooms at the front and all manner of artefacts beyond; don't miss the Art Nouveau furniture.

Lunch. See page 115. Take lunch at the idiosyncratic *Maison Elza*, where, if the weather holds, you can eat out on the pontoon at the back.

Het Gravensteen. See page 104. Sullen and stern, the cold stone walls of Ghent's castle dominate this part of the city centre. Inside, there' a series of exhibitions about the medieval city.

Huis van Alijn. See page 106. Get to grips with the traditional culture of Flanders, from funerary rights and religious processions to celebrations and street games.

Dinner. See page 115. Ghent has a great restaurant – to try traditional Flemish ad for *De Lieve*.

page 117. Round off with a few beers – the *aan de Bierkant* will

The vaulted nave in St-Baafskathedraal

Medieval guild houses on the Graslei

The Design Museum

Day Two in Ghent

MSK. See page 120. Art-lovers will want to make a bee line for this excellent museum, which holds a prestigious collection of Belgian art from the Flemish Primitives right through to Paul Delvaux and René Magritte.

S.M.A.K. See page 119. Not for the artistically squeamish, perhaps, but this capacious museum has a reputation for its adventurous sometimes shocking exhibitions of contemporary art, featuring works from every corner of the globe.

Citadelpark. See page 119. Ghent is oh-so-very flat, so the wooded hillocks of this large park come as a pleasant change – and its assorted fountains, grottoes and statues are an agreeable scenic surprise.

Lunch. See page 121. *Vooruit* may not be a gourmet's paradise, but it is the cultural centre of the city, especially for Ghent's university students. It's barn-like café-bar serves up filling snacks and light meals at very affordable prices.

St-Baafsabdij. See page 124. Well off the beaten track, the evocative ruins of this ancient abbey are truly delightful and incorporate an ivy-covered Gothic cloister and all manner of finely carved architectural bits and bobs: gargoyles, terracotta panels, capitals, columns and so forth.

Dinner. See page 127. *Martino* is Ghent at its liveliest, a busy, bustling diner where the steaks and burgers are first rate and the house speciality is the Martino comprising raw beef with mustard, Tabasco, tomato and anchovy.

A gallery at MSK

Citadelpark

St-Baafsabdij

Art in Bruges

When it comes to medieval art, Bruges packs well above its weight. The big-name galleries attract the most attention, but the churches and smaller museums are worth seeking out.

St-Jakobskerk. See page 70. The walls of this handsome church display more than eighty paintings gifted by the city's merchants. The pick are two finely executed triptychs dating from the late-fifteenth century.

St-Walburgakerk. See page 75. The Jesuits of the seventeenth century had a Counter Reformation point to make when they built St-Walburgakerk, a Baroque extravagance complete with Pieter Claeissen the Younger's triptych celebrating Philip the Good, one-time count of Flanders.

St-Annakerk. See page 76. This dinky little church, with its slender brick tower, may look restrained from the outside, but the interior holds a huge and gaudy *Last Judgement* by the itinerant artist Hendrik Herregouts.

🍽 Lunch. See page 87. No argument, *Café Vlissinghe* is one of the most charming café-bars in Bruges, all wood-panelling and long tables. The food is simple Flemish fare at competitive prices.

Museum Onze-Lieve-Vrouw-ter-Potterie. See page 82. This intimate museum occupies a one-time medieval hospital. The old sick room displays a charming assortment of medieval religious ~~paintings~~, most memorably a ~~carving~~ panel-painting of *St ~~Michael~~ triumphing over the Devil.*

~~Dinner.~~ See page 86. Stay ~~on the~~ northern side of the ~~...~~ or an excellent meal at

Detail from a painting at St-Jakobskerk

The altar at St-Walburgakerk

Museum Onze-Lieve-Vrouw-ter-Potterie

A drinker's day in Bruges

The key to enjoying and exploring Bruges's delightful bars is to pace yourself – and pay close attention to the alcohol percentage on the beer bottle or draft pump.

Bourgogne des Flandres. See page 43. Make a leisurely start with this brewery tour, which provides an introduction to the brewing process. Afterwards, you'll get a bottle of their classic red-brown beer to quaff.

De Garre. See page 45. Down a narrow alley, this ancient tavern is a real delight with a wide-ranging beer menu plus jazz and classical music.

Lunch. See page 44. Just off the Burg, the friendly *Gulliver Tree* does a good line in light lunches – toasties, salads and soups – in amenable surroundings.

Bourgogne des Flandres brewery

Café Rose Red. See page 45. This smart little place has the full-range of Trappist beers from all six of Belgium's monkish breweries: Achel, Chimay, Orval, Rochefort, Westmalle and Westvleteren.

Café Craenenburg. See page 34. One of the few café-bars on the Markt to retain a local clientele, the Craenenburg has the flavour of old Flanders with its antique benches and mullion windows.

Café Craenenburg

The Bottle Shop. See page 44. Every Belgian beer you can think of and then some is on sale here at this bright and cheerful shop; there is a wide selection of jenever too.

Dinner. See page 45. Arguably the best seafood restaurant in town, *De Visscherie* is smart, expensive and enjoyable; the sole and the mussels are house specialities.

The Bottle Shop

PLACES

View from the Belfort, Bruges

The Markt

To the surprise of many first-time visitors, Bruges is not the perfectly preserved medieval city described by much tourist literature, but rather a clever, frequently seamless combination of medieval original and nineteenth- and even twentieth-century additions. This is especially true of the city's principal square, the Markt, an airy open space fringed by pavement cafés where horse-drawn buggies clatter over the square's cobbles and tourists mill around. It's overlooked to the south by the imposing Belfort (belfry), long the city's proudest landmark. There's also much to admire on the north and west sides of the Markt, which are flanked by a charming ensemble of biscuit-tin buildings with mellow ruddy-brown brick culminating in a string of gables, each slightly different from its neighbour. This isn't a planned confection, but a sympathetic rehashing of what went before. The Markt's east side is all Neo-Gothic, with the thunderous facade of the old provincial government building announced by a brace of stone lions.

Biscuit-tin buildings on the Markt

Monument to Pieter de Coninck and Jan Breydel

MAP P.30, POCKET MAP C5
Markt.

The burghers of nineteenth-century Bruges were keen to put something suitably civic in the middle of the Markt and the result is the conspicuous **monument** to Pieter de Coninck, of the guild of weavers, and Jan Breydel, dean of the guild of butchers. Standing close together, they clutch the hilt of the same sword, their faces turned to the south in slightly absurd poses of heroic determination – a far cry from the gory events that first made them local heroes. At dawn on Friday, May 18, 1302, in what was later called the **Bruges Matins**, their force of rebellious Flemings crept into the city and massacred the unsuspecting French garrison, putting to the sword anyone who couldn't correctly pronounce the Flemish shibboleth *schild en vriend*

Monument to Pieter de Coninck and Jan Breydel

("shield and friend"). Later the same year, the two guildsmen went on to lead the city's contingent in the Flemish army that defeated the French at the Battle of the Golden Spurs – no surprise, then, that the monument takes its cue from the battle rather than the massacre. Curiously enough, the statue was unveiled twice: in July 1887, a local committee pulled back the drapes to celebrate Coninck and Breydel as Flemings, whilst in August of the same year the city council organized an official opening, when King Leopold II honoured them as Belgians.

Provinciaal Hof

MAP P.30, POCKET MAP C5
Markt 3. No public access.

Hogging the eastern side of the Markt is the former provincial government building, the **Provinciaal Hof**, a fancy if over-large Neo-Gothic edifice whose assorted spires, balustrades and dormer windows took forty years

The museum pass

The **Museum Pass**, which is valid for three days, covers entry to all the main museums and costs €20 (12–25 year olds €15; ⓦ visitbruges.be/practical-information). Fourteen municipal museums are covered including the Belfort, the Stadhuis, the Arentshuis, the Groeninge, the Gruuthuse, Onze Lieve Vrouwekerk and St-Janshospitaalmuseum. Depending on exactly which museums you visit, the pass can offer a significant saving compared to buying individual tickets. Sites not covered by the pass include St-Salvatorskathedraal and gimmicky new attractions like the **Historium**, on the Markt, where you can don virtual reality goggles to "visit" medieval Bruges. Museum passes can be bought at any of the fourteen participants, as well as from the tourist office (see page 5); note that most of the museums are closed on Mondays.

Provinciaal Hof

to complete. They were finally finished in 1921. The smaller building immediately to the left is also Neo-Gothic, added in the 1920s and complete with twin arcaded galleries.

Café Craenenburg

MAP P.30, POCKET MAP C5
Markt 16.

Today, the **Café Craenenburg** (see page 34) occupies a relatively undistinguished modern building on the corner of St-Amandsstraat, but this was the site of the eponymous medieval mansion in which the guildsmen of Bruges imprisoned the Habsburg heir, Archduke Maximilian, for three months in 1488. The reason for their difference of opinion was the archduke's efforts to limit the city's privileges, but whatever the justice of their cause, the guildsmen made a big mistake. Maximilian made all sorts of promises to escape their clutches, but a few weeks after his release his father, the Emperor Frederick III, turned up with an army to take imperial revenge, with a bit of hanging here and a bit of burning there. Maximilian became emperor in 1493 and never

CAFÉS	
Café Craenenburg	3
Lb DbB	6
Sorbetiere de Medici	2

RESTAURANTS	
Den Amand	4
In Den Wittenkop	1
De Stove	5

The Markt

Stadsschouwburg

Bibliotheek

Monument to Pieter de Coninck and Jan Breydel

MARKT

Provinciaal Hof

Café Craenenburg

Belfort

Hallen

SHOPS	
De Corte	3
Diksmuids Boterhuis	2
INNO	8
Olivier's Chocolate Shop	4
Proxy Noordzand	5
Reisboekhandel	6
De Reyghere	7
Think Twice	1

The bells, the bells

Bruges still employs a full-time bell-ringer and you're likely to spot him or her fiddling around in the **Belfort's Carillon Room** (see page 32) as s/he prepares for one of the city's regular **carillon concerts** (currently Wed, Sat & Sun at 11am; plus mid-June to mid-Sept Mon & Wed at 9pm). Like in other Flemish cities, **bells** were first used in Bruges in the fourteenth century as a means of regulating the working day, and as such reflected the development of a wage economy – employers were keen to keep tabs on their employees. Bells also served as a sort of public address system with everyone understanding the signals: pealing bells, for example, announced good news; tolling bells summoned the city to the Markt; and a rapid sequence of bells warned of danger. By the early fifteenth century a short peal of bells marked the hour, and from this developed the carillon (beiaard), with Bruges installing its present version in the middle of the eighteenth century.

forgave Bruges, not only failing to honour his promises but also doing his considerable best to push trade north to its great rival, Antwerp.

Belfort

MAP P.30, POCKET MAP C6
Markt 7 ☎ 050 44 87 43, ⓦ visitbruges.be.
Daily 9.30am–6pm, last admission 5pm.
€12. Entry via the Hallen (see page 32).
Filling out the south side of the Markt, the mighty **Belfort** (belfry) was long a potent symbol of civic pride and municipal independence, its distinctive octagonal lantern visible for miles across the surrounding polders. The Belfort was begun in the thirteenth century, when the town was at its richest and most extravagant, but it has had a blighted history beginning when the original wooden version was struck by lightning and burnt to the ground in 1280. Its brick replacement, with today's blind arcading, turrets and towers, received its octagonal stone lantern and a second wooden spire in the 1480s, but this spire didn't last long either, being lost to a thunderstorm a few years later. Undeterred, the Flemings promptly added a third spire, though when this went

up in smoke in 1741 the locals gave up, settling for the present structure with the addition of a stone parapet in 1822. It's a pity they didn't have another go, if only to sabotage Longfellow's metre in his dire but oft-quoted poem *The Belfry of Bruges*: "In the market place of Bruges/Stands the Belfry old and brown/Thrice consumed and thrice rebuilt …", and so

Belfort

The Carillon Chamber at the top of the Belfort

on. Few would say the Belfort is good-looking – it's large and really rather clumsy – but it does have a certain ungainly charm. However, this was lost on G.K. Chesterton, who described it as "an unnaturally long-necked animal, like a giraffe".

Inside, the **belfry staircase** begins innocuously enough, but gets steeper and much narrower as it nears the top. On the way up, it passes several mildly interesting chambers, beginning with the **Treasury Room**, where the town charters and money chest were locked for safe keeping. Here also is an iron trumpet with which a watchman could warn the town of a fire outbreak – though given the size of the instrument, it's hard to believe this was very effective. Further up is the **Carillon Chamber**, a small and intimate cubby hole, where you can observe the slow turning of the large spiked drum that controls the 47 bells of the municipal carillon (see page 31); the largest bell weighs no less than six tonnes. A few stairs up from here and you emerge onto the **roof**, which offers fabulous views, especially in the late afternoon when the warm colours of the city are at their deepest.

Hallen

MAP P.30, POCKET MAP C6
Markt 7. Open access. Free.

The **Hallen** at the foot of the belfry is a much-restored thirteenth-century edifice, whose austere style and structure were modelled on the Lakenhalle in Ieper (see page 99). In the middle, overlooked by a long line of former warehouses, is a rectangular courtyard, which originally served as the city's principal market, its cobblestones once crammed with merchants and their wares, trading anything and everything from gloves, carpets, clerical hats and clogs through to fruits and spices. The entrance to the belfry (see page 31) is on the north side of the courtyard, up a flight of steps, while other parts of the Hallen are used for exhibitions geared up for the passing tourist trade. Incidentally, the gloomy set of arches to the rear of the Hallen, beyond the courtyard, was once the preserve of the money-changers, who had to deal with a bewildering variety of currencies in coins that might be clipped or debased as the issuers regularly varied the content. The development of a reliable banking industry was key to the prosperity of medieval Bruges.

Shops

De Corte

MAP P.30, POCKET MAP C5
Sint-Amandsstraat 28 ☎ 050 33 46 07,
Ⓦ decortebrugge.be. Tues–Fri 9.30am–
12.30pm & 1.30–6pm, Sat 9.30am–6pm.
Smart little shop in a handy
location selling a premium selection
of pens, notebooks, inks, bags and
Swiss army knives. The Montblanc
pens, one of the shop's specialities,
attract well-heeled customers.

Diksmuids Boterhuis

MAP P.30, POCKET MAP C5
Geldmuntstraat 23 ☎ 050 33 32 43,
Ⓦ diksmuidsboterhuis.be. Tues–Sat
9.30am–12.30pm & 2–6.30pm.
One of the few traditional food
shops to have survived in central
Bruges, this Aladdin's cave of a
place specializes in cooked meats,
breads, butters and Belgian cheeses,
of which it has an outstanding
selection. Friendly service, too

INNO

MAP P.30, POCKET MAP C6
Steenstraat 13 ☎ 050 33 06 03, Ⓦ services.
inno.be. Mon–Sat 9.30am–6pm.

The best department store in the
city centre spread over four large
floors. The ground floor sells
watches, perfume, make-up, bags
and lingerie, while the other floors
are largely devoted to good-quality
clothes, for both men and women
and divided up into leading brands.

Olivier's Chocolate Shop

MAP P.30, POCKET MAP C5
Sint-Amandsstraat 14 ☎ 050 73 22 60,
Ⓦ olivierschocolate.be. Daily 11am–
6.30pm.
Bruges has accumulated a small
army of specialist chocolate
shops in recent years, but this
family-owned concern has won
rave reviews for the quality of
its chocolate. The shop is in a
handy central location; it's nicely
presented and sells the (slightly)
larger and more traditional type of
Belgian chocolate.

Proxy Noordzand

MAP P.30, POCKET MAP B5
Noordzandstraat 4 ☎ 050 34 16 12,
Ⓦ delhaize.be. Mon–Sat 8am–7.30pm.
Ordinary shops and stores have
all but vanished from central
Bruges, but there are a couple of

Diksmuids Boterhuis

smallish supermarkets – and this is perhaps the best. Nothing fancy, but a reliable selection of fresh veg, cooked meats and so forth.

Reisboekhandel

MAP P.30, POCKET MAP C5
Markt 13 ☏ 050 49 12 29, ⓦ dereyghere.
be. Mon 12.30–6pm & Tues–Sat
9.30am–12.30pm & 1.30–6pm.
Travel specialist with a wide selection of travel guides, many in English, plus road and city maps. The shop also sells hiking and cycling maps of Bruges and its surroundings, and stocks travel-related English-language magazines. Next door you'll find its sister shop, De Reyghere (see below).

De Reyghere

MAP P.30, POCKET MAP C6
Markt 12 ☏ 050 33 34 03, ⓦ dereyghere.
be. Mon–Sat 9am–6pm.
Founded more than one hundred years ago, De Reyghere is something of a local institution and a meeting place for every book-lover in town. The shop stocks a wide range of domestic and foreign

Think Twice

literature, art and reference books, and is also good for international newspapers, magazines and periodicals.

Think Twice

MAP P.30, POCKET MAP C5
St-Jakobsstraat 21 ☏ 0495 36 39 08,
ⓦ thinktwice-secondhand.be/shops/
vintage-shop-brugge. Mon–Sat 10am–6pm
& Sun 1–5pm.
Part of a well-intentioned chain of Belgian stores – there are nine in total – in which second-hand clothes are collected, sorted and re-sold at budget prices. This particular outlet sells mostly women's wear, from shoes, hats and dresses through to coats and bags.

Cafés

Café Craenenburg

MAP P.30, POCKET MAP C5
Markt 16 ☏ 050 33 34 02, ⓦ craenenburg.
be. Mon–Fri 8am–11pm, Sat 8.30am–11pm.
Unlike the Markt's other café-restaurants, this traditional place still attracts a loyal, local clientele. With its leather and wood panelling, antique benches and mullion windows, the *Craenenburg* has the flavour of old Flanders, and although the daytime-only food is routine (mains average €20), it has a good range of beers, including a locally produced, tangy brown ale called *Brugse Tripel*.

Lb DbB

MAP P.30, POCKET MAP C6
Kleine St-Amandsstraat 5 ☏ 050 34 91
31, ⓦ debelegdeboterham.be. Mon–Sat
11.30am–4pm.
An outstanding café, this bright and breezy little place, in attractively renovated premises down a narrow lane, has a strong local following on account of its wonderfully substantial and absolutely delicious salads (€16). The service is prompt and friendly too. By some measure, it's the best place to eat in the vicinity of the Markt.

In Den Wittenkop

Sorbetiere de Medici

MAP P.30, POCKET MAP C5
Geldmuntstraat 9 ☎ 050 33 93 41,
Ⓦ demedici.be. Mon 1–5pm, Tues–Sat
9am–5pm.

An enjoyable antidote to the
plain modernism of many of its
rivals, this attractive café boasts
an extravagantly ornate interior,
complete with a huge mirror and
spindly curving staircase. It also
serves great coffee plus tasty pastas
and salads, but these are as nothing
compared to the hot dessert pies
– the almond with red berry juice
will have you aching with delight.

Restaurants

Den Amand

MAP P.30, POCKET MAP C5
St-Amandsstraat 4 ☎ 050 34 01 22,
Ⓦ denamand.be. Mon, Tues & Thurs–Sat
noon–2.15pm & 6–9pm.

Decorated in pleasant modern style,
this small and informal, family-run
restaurant offers an inventive range
of dishes combining Flemish, Italian
and even Asian cuisines. Mains from
the limited but well-chosen menu
– for instance, brill in coconut milk
– average a very reasonable €22. It's

a small place, so best to book a few
hours in advance.

In Den Wittenkop

MAP P.30, POCKET MAP C5
St-Jakobsstraat 14 ☎ 050 33 20 59,
Ⓦ indenwittenkop.be. Mon, Tues & Thurs–
Sat noon–3pm & 6–10pm.

This cosy restaurant with its
hotchpotch decor specializes in
traditional Flemish dishes – try,
for example, the rabbit in prunes
or the local speciality of pork and
beef stewed in Trappist beer. There's
smooth jazz as background music
and a small terrace out the back.
Mains average €24, €15 for the
dish of the day.

De Stove

MAP P.30, POCKET MAP C6
Kleine St-Amandsstraat 4 ☎ 050 33 78
35, Ⓦ restaurantdestove.be. Mon, Tues &
Fri–Sat 7–10pm, Sun noon–2pm & 7–10pm.

Small and cosy Franco-Belgian
restaurant that's recommended by
just about everyone. The menu is
carefully constructed, with both
fish and meat dishes given equal
prominence. À la carte mains cost
around €30, but the big deal is the
three-course set menu for €52 (€70
with wine). Reservations essential.

The Burg

Named after the ninth-century fortress built here by the first count of Flanders, Baldwin Iron Arm, the Burg is the city's architectural showpiece. It's a handsome square whose southern edge is flanked by an especially beguiling mix of late-Gothic and Renaissance buildings, including Bruges's holy of holies, the Heilig Bloed Basiliek (Basilica of the Holy Blood). The fortress disappeared centuries ago, but the Burg long remained the centre of political and ecclesiastical power with the Stadhuis (Town Hall), which has survived, on one side and St-Donaaskathedraal, which hasn't, on the other. The French Revolutionary army destroyed the cathedral in 1799 and, although the foundations were laid bare a few years ago, they were promptly re-interred and now lie in front of and underneath the Crowne Plaza Hotel.

Heilig Bloed Basiliek

MAP P.38, POCKET MAP D6
Burg 13 ☏ 050 33 67 92, ⓦ holyblood.
com. April–Oct daily 9.30am–12.30pm &
2–5.30pm; Nov–March Mon, Tues & Thurs–
Sun 9.30am–12.30pm & 2–5.30pm, Wed
9.30am–12.30pm. Free, but treasury €2.50.

Heilig Bloed Basiliek

Once a celebrated place of pilgrimage, the **Heilig Bloed Basiliek** (Basilica of the Holy Blood) is named after the holy relic that found its way here in the Middle Ages – a rock-crystal phial that purports to contain a few drops of blood and water washed from the body of Christ by Joseph of Arimathea (see page 37). The basilica divides into two parts. Tucked away in the corner is the **lower chapel**, a shadowy, crypt-like affair that was originally built at the start of the twelfth century to shelter another relic, a piece of St Basil who was one of the great figures of the early Greek Church. The chapel's heavy and simple Romanesque lines are decorated with just one relief, carved above an interior doorway and showing the baptism of Basil, in which a strange giant bird, representing the Holy Spirit, plunges into a pool of water.

Next door, approached up a low-vaulted, curving staircase, is the **upper chapel**, which was built just a few years later, but has been renovated so frequently that it's impossible to make out the original structure – and it also suffers from an excess of kitsch nineteenth-century decoration. The chapel itself may be disappointing, but the large silver **tabernacle** that holds the phial of the Holy Blood is simply magnificent. It was the gift of Albert and Isabella of Spain in 1611. The Habsburg King Philip II of Spain had granted control of the Spanish Netherlands (now Belgium) to his daughter Isabella and her husband Albert in 1598, but they were imprudent rulers, exalting the Catholic faith – as per the tabernacle – whilst simultaneously persecuting those Protestants who remained in their fiefdom.

Beside the upper chapel is the tiny **Schatkamer** (treasury), where pride of place goes to the ornate shrine that holds the holy phial during the Heilig-Bloedprocessie. Dating from 1617, it's a superb piece of work, the gold-and-silver,

The main altar at the Heilig Bloed Basiliek

The holiest of holies: the Holy Blood

Local legend asserts that the phial of the **Heilig Bloed** (Holy Blood) was the gift of Diederik d'Alsace, a Flemish count who distinguished himself by his bravery during the Second Crusade and was given the relic by a grateful patriarch of Jerusalem in 1150. It is, however, rather more likely that the phial was acquired during the sacking of Constantinople in 1204, when the Crusaders ignored their collective job description and, instead of attacking the Moslem rulers of Palestine, slaughtered the Byzantines instead – hence the historical invention. Whatever the truth, after several weeks in Bruges the relic was found to be dry, but thereafter the dried blood proceeded to liquefy every Friday at 6pm until 1325, a miracle attested to by all sorts of church dignitaries, including Pope Clement V. After 1325, the failure of the Holy Blood to liquefy prompted all sorts of conjecture – did it mean that Bruges had lost favour in the eyes of God? – but the phial, or more exactly its dried contents, remain an object of veneration today. It's sometimes available for visitors to touch under the supervision of a priest in the upper chapel, and on Ascension Day (mid-May) it's carried through the town in a colourful but solemn procession, the **Heilig-Bloedprocessie** (Procession of the Holy Blood; ⓦ bloedprocessiebrugge.be/en). The procession usually starts on Wollestraat at 2.30pm and then wends its way round the centre before finishing off at around 6pm. Grandstand tickets (€12) are sold online and at the main tourist office (see page 145) from March 1.

Statue of Christ at the Heilig Bloed Basiliek

jewel-encrusted superstructure decorated with delicate religious scenes. The treasury also contains an incidental collection of vestments and lesser reliquaries plus a handful of late medieval paintings, most memorably a finely executed pair of panels by Pieter Pourbus depicting the thirty-one *Members of the Noble Brotherhood of the Precious Blood*. Born in Gouda, in the Netherlands, Pourbus (1523–84) moved to Bruges when he was a young man and it was here he established a reputation for the quality of his portrait painting, his closely observed figures very much in the Netherlandish tradition. Less polished, but equally charming, is a naïve panel-painting entitled *Scenes from the Life of St Barbara* by the Master of the St Barbara Legend. A hazy third-century figure, Barbara was supposedly imprisoned in a tower by her pagan father, who subsequently tortured and killed her on account of her Christian faith; the tower became Barbara's symbol and is shown here under construction. Finally, look out for the faded strands of

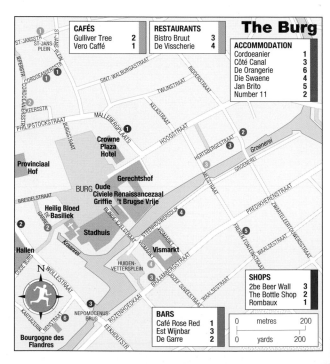

The Burg

CAFÉS
Gulliver Tree 2
Vero Caffé 1

RESTAURANTS
Bistro Bruut 3
De Visscherie 4

ACCOMMODATION
Cordoeanier 1
Côté Canal 3
De Orangerie 6
Die Swaene 4
Jan Brito 5
Number 11 2

SHOPS
2be Beer Wall 3
The Bottle Shop 2
Rombaux 1

BARS
Café Rose Red 1
Est Wijnbar 3
De Garre 2

a seventeenth-century tapestry depicting St Augustine's funeral, the sea of helmeted heads, torches and pikes that surround the monks and abbots very much a Catholic view of a muscular State supporting a holy Church.

Stadhuis

MAP P.38, POCKET MAP D6
Burg 12 ☎ 050 44 87 43, ⓦ visitbruges.
be. Daily 9.30am–5pm. €6, including the
Renaissancezaal (see page 40).

The **Stadhuis** (Town Hall), just to the left of the basilica, has a beautiful sandstone facade of 1376, though its statues, mostly of the counts and countesses of Flanders, are modern replacements for those destroyed by the occupying French army in 1792. Inside, a flight of stairs clambers up from the high-ceilinged foyer to the magnificent **Gothic Hall**, dating from 1400 and the setting for the first meeting of the States General (parliamentary assembly) in 1464. The ceiling here has been restored in a vibrant mixture of maroon, dark brown, black and gold – dripping pendant arches like decorated stalactites. The ribs

of the arches converge in twelve circular **vault-keys**, picturing scenes from the New Testament. These are hard to see without binoculars, but down below – and much easier to view – are the sixteen gilded **corbels** that support them, representing the months and the four elements, beginning in the left-hand corner beside the chimney with January (inscribed "Winter") and continuing clockwise right round the hall. The wall **frescoes** were commissioned in 1895 to illustrate the history of the town – or rather history as the council were keen to recall it. The largest scene, commemorating the victory over the French at the Battle of the Golden Spurs in 1302, has lots of knights hurrahing, though it's hard to take this seriously when you look at the dogs, one of which clearly has a mismatch between its body and head. Finally, adjoining the Gothic Hall is the unassuming **Historische zaal** (Historical Room), which holds a mildly diverting display of municipal artefacts, including two finely drawn, sixteenth-century city maps.

Stadhuis

Oude Civiele Griffie

Oude Civiele Griffie

MAP P.38, POCKET MAP D6
Burg 11. No public access.

Next door to the Stadhuis, the bright and cheery **Oude Civiele Griffie** (Old Civic Registry) was built to house the municipal records office in 1537, its elegant facade decorated with Renaissance columns and friezes. The gable features half a dozen gold-painted statues – three representations of civic virtues positioned slightly below Moses and Aaron with the blindfolded figure of Justice and her scales plonked right on the top. The building also spans the archway over **Blinde Ezelstraat** (Blind Donkey Street), whose name has attracted all sorts of speculation (see page 43).

Renaissancezaal 't Brugse Vrije

MAP P.38, POCKET MAP D5
Burg 11A ☎ 050 44 87 43, ⓦ visitbruges. be. Daily 9.30am–12.30pm & 1.30–5pm. €6, including Stadhuis (see page 39).

Adjacent to the Oude Civiele Griffie, the **Landhuis van het**

Brugse Vrije (Mansion of the Liberty of Bruges) is demure in comparison but it boasts a distinguished history. Established in the Middle Ages, the Liberty of Bruges was a territorial subdivision of Flanders that enjoyed extensive delegated powers, controlling its own finances and judiciary. A council of aldermen exercised power and it was they who demolished most of the original Gothic building in the early eighteenth century, before Napoleon abolished them. Just one room has survived from the original structure, the Schepenkamer (Aldermen's Room), now known as the **Renaissancezaal 't Brugse Vrije** (Renaissance Hall of the Liberty of Bruges). Dominating the room is an enormous marble and oak chimneypiece, a superb example of Renaissance carving completed in 1531 to celebrate the defeat of the French at Pavia six years earlier and the advantageous Treaty of Cambrai that followed. A paean of praise to the Habsburgs, the work features the Emperor Charles V and his Austrian and Spanish relatives, though it's the trio of bulbous (and presumably exceptionally uncomfortable) **codpieces** that really catches the eye. The **alabaster frieze** running below the carvings was a caution for the Liberty's magistrates, who held their courts here. In four panels, it relates the then-familiar biblical story of **Susanna**, in which – in the first panel – two old men surprise her bathing in her garden and threaten to accuse her of adultery if she resists their advances. Susanna does just that, and the second panel shows her in court. In the third panel, Susanna is about to be put to death, but the magistrate, Daniel, interrogates the two men and uncovers their perjury. Susanna is acquitted and, in the final scene, the two men are stoned to death.

Grim tidings: the murder of Charles the Good

In 1127, **St-Donaaskathedraal** (see page 42) witnessed an event that shocked the whole of western Europe, when the Count of Flanders, **Charles the Good** (1084–1127), was murdered while he was at prayer in the choir. A gifted and far-sighted ruler, Charles eschewed foreign entanglements in favour of domestic matters – unlike most of his predecessors – and improved the lot of the poor by both trying to ensure a regular supply of food and controlling prices in times of shortage. These far-sighted policies, along with his personal piety, earned Charles his sobriquet, but the count's attempts to curb his leading vassals brought him into conflict with the powerful Erembald clan. The Erembalds had no intention of submitting to Charles, so they assassinated him and took control of the city. Their success was, however, short-lived. Supporters of Charles rallied and the murderers took refuge in the tower of St Donatian's, from where they were winkled out and promptly dispatched. Shocked by the murder, one of Charles's clerks, a certain **Galbert of Bruges**, decided to write a detailed journal of the events that led up to the assassination and the bloody chaos that ensued. Unlike other contemporary source materials, the journal had no sponsor, which makes it a uniquely honest account of events, admittedly from the perspective of the count's entourage, with Galbert criticizing many of the city's leading figures, clergy and nobles alike. Galbert's journal provides a fascinating insight into twelfth-century Bruges and it's well written too (in a wordy sort of way) – as in the account of Charles' death: "when the count was praying ... then at last, after so many plans and oaths and pacts among themselves, those wretched traitors ... slew the count, who was struck down with swords and run through again and again". The full text is reprinted in The Murder of Charles the Good, edited by James Bruce Ross.

The carved chimneypiece at the Renaissancezaal 't Brugse Vrije

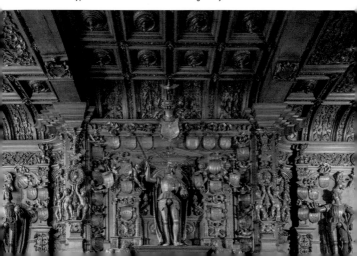

Blinde Ezelstraat

Gerechtshof

MAP P.38, POCKET MAP D5
Burg 9. No public access.

At the eastern corner of the Burg is the Neoclassical **Gerechtshof** (Law Courts), a substantial sandstone complex surrounding a large cobbled courtyard. It was built in the 1720s as part of an attempt to streamline the administration of justice in Bruges and remained in use as a law court until 1984; it's now home to municipal offices. One of the most dramatic cases heard here was that of **Ludovicus Baekelandt**, a rough-and-tumble Fleming who joined the invading French army in 1794 and then deserted to become an outlaw preying on travellers from his forest hideout. Baekelandt's activities made him something of a folk hero among his fellow Flemings, many of whom were deeply resentful of the French, but he and his gang were caught in 1802 and brought to Bruges, where twenty-four of them were tried and guillotined in the Markt. A large and sullen crowd watched the proceedings.

St-Donaaskathedraal

MAP P.38, POCKET MAP D5
Burg.

On the corner of the Burg, the modern *Crowne Plaza* hotel marks the site of the east end of **St-Donaaskathedraal** (St Donatian's Cathedral), which was razed by the French army of occupation in 1799. By all accounts the church was a splendid structure, a mighty Romanesque edifice dating from the tenth century with a lantern tower and a sixteen-sided ambulatory. To the French Revolutionary army, however, it was a symbol of religious superstition and of the reactionary city council, whose burghers had long held sway. Neither was the church's demolition a passing fancy: the French arrived with a team of demolition experts, who began by jacking up the church roof and inserting timber blocks in the gaps. They then set fire to the wood so that the building literally collapsed into itself, leaving a great pile of rubble that took decades to clear. The cathedral's foundations were uncovered in 1955 but were then reinterred and, although there are vague plans to carry out another archeological dig, nothing has happened yet.

The Vismarkt and around

MAP P.38, POCKET MAP D6

The arch beside the Stadhuis marks the start of **Blinde Ezelstraat** (Blind Donkey Street), whose name has been the subject of much debate: one story suggests that donkeys coming along here were blindfolded in case they got spooked by the narrowness of the street, but it's more likely that the name refers to an old and long-gone tavern which sold the cheapest booze in town and whose clientele ended up as drunk as "blind donkeys". Whatever the truth, Blinde Ezelstraat now leads south across the canal to the plain and sombre, early nineteenth-century Doric colonnades of the **Vismarkt** (fish market), though, with its handful of fish traders, this is but a shadow of its former self. Neither are there any tanners in the huddle of picturesque houses that crimp the **Huidenvettersplein**, the square at the centre of the old tanners' quarter immediately to the west – a good job as the locals of yesteryear often complained of the stench. Tourists converge on this pint-sized square in their droves, holing up in its bars and restaurants and snapping away at the postcard-perfect views of the belfry from the adjacent **Rozenhoedkaai** – literally "rosary quay", named after the amber and ivory rosaries that were a speciality of the craftsmen who worked here until the nineteenth century.

Nepomucenusbrug

MAP P.38, POCKET MAP D6

The **Nepomucenusbrug**, at the junction of Rozenhoedkaai and Wollestraat, sports a statue of the patron saint of bridges, St John Nepomuk, a fourteenth-century Bohemian priest who was purportedly thrown bound and gagged into the River Vltava for refusing to reveal the confessional secrets of the queen to her husband, King Wenceslas IV. The bridge marks the start of the **Dijver**, which tracks along the canal as far as Nieuwstraat, passing the path to the first of the city's main museums, the Groeninge (see page 50).

Bourgogne des Flandres

MAP P.38, POCKET MAP C6

Kartuizerinnenstraat 6, off Wollestraat
T 32 50 33 54 26, W bourgognedesflandres.be. Tues–Sun 10am–6pm. Guided tours every 20min, 40min. €10.50.

Pleased to have finally returned to Bruges, the **Bourgogne des Flandres brewery** occupies a pair of attractive brick buildings on a narrow side-street just off Wollestraat. Guided tours include a quick introduction to the brewing process, a gander at the brewing equipment in the loft and, at the end of the tour, a bottle of the stuff to quaff. Bourgogne des Flandres is a classic red-brown beer blended with eight-month-old lambic that is produced by the brewery's owners, the Brussels-based Timmermans Brewery.

Statue of St. John of Nepomuk

Shops

2be Beer Wall

MAP P.38, POCKET MAP D6
Wollestraat 53 ☏ 050 61 12 22, ⓦ 2-be.biz.
Daily 10am–7pm.

Stroll through the old arch at
the foot of Wollestraat and you
are faced – quite literally – with
a wall of Belgian beer bottles;
take your pick and pay up.
Alternatively, you can quaff
your selection at the adjoining
bar, which is short of creature
comforts but does have a wide
range of beers. Hence, it's a very
popular tourist spot.

The Bottle Shop

MAP P.38, POCKET MAP C6
Wollestraat 13 ☏ 050 34 99 80,
ⓦ thebottleshop.be. Daily
10am–6.30pm.

Just off the Markt this bright and
cheerful establishment stocks more
than six hundred types of beer,
oodles of whisky and *jenever* (gin),
as well as all sorts of special glasses
to drink them from. The Belgians
have specific glasses for many of
their beers.

2be Beer Wall

Rombaux

MAP P.38, POCKET MAP D5
Mallebergplaats 13 ☏ 050 33 25 75,
ⓦ rombaux.be. Mon 2–6.30pm, Tues–Fri
10am–12.30pm & 2–6.30pm & Sat
10am–6pm.

This is actually two adjacent shops:
one selling musical instruments,
especially pianos and organs, the
other with an enormous collection
of CDs covering every musical
taste, including an especially good
selection of jazz and classical music.

Cafés

Gulliver Tree

MAP P.38, POCKET MAP C5
Cordoeaniersstraat 4 ☏ 050 73 15 16,
ⓦ thegullivertree.be. Tues–Sat 9am–5pm.

Just off the Burg, this cosy, friendly
café is more spacious than most
of its rivals – and is all the better
for that. The coffee is good, there
is a wide range of teas and herbal
infusions. At lunchtime (noon–
2pm) they serve up tasty toasties,
salads and soup.

Vero Caffé

MAP P.38, POCKET MAP C5
St-Jansplein 9 ☏ 050 70 96 09. Daily
11am–6pm.

A simply decorated café with
whitewashed brick walls where local
hipsters and students rub shoulders
to enjoy a particularly good cup
of coffee. There are home-baked
cakes too, but the tastiest disappear
early. Its location on a quiet square
is pleasantly removed from the
hubbub of central Bruges.

Restaurants

Bistro Bruut

MAP P.38, POCKET MAP D5
Meestraat 9 ☏ 050 69 55 09, ⓦ bistrobruut.
be. Mon–Fri noon–2.30pm & 7–9.30pm.

Head down a narrow, ancient side
street close to the Burg and you'll
find, overlooking a canal, this
tastefully decorated bistro with

a retro feel (love that black and white chequerboard floor!). The chef chooses the menu – you just choose the number of courses you want, up to a maximum of five or six. The menu is an elaboration of traditional Flemish cuisine with due emphasis on seasonal, organic ingredients. Try the lobster tartare with Brussels sprouts. A starter and main course costs €30. Reservations essential.

De Visscherie

MAP P.38, POCKET MAP D6
Vismarkt 8 ☎ 050 33 02 12, ⓦ visscherie.be. Daily except Tues & Wed noon–2pm & 7–10pm.
Arguably the city's premier seafood restaurant, *De Visscherie* is a smooth, smart and polished restaurant with a good reputation. A well-presented and creative menu features such delights as a spectacularly tasty fish soup and monkfish in a beer sauce. Mains are, however, expensive – reckon on €42. The restaurant occupies the ground floor of a spacious nineteenth-century mansion a short walk south of the Burg, but the decor has some intriguing modern touches – small sculptures and so on – and the chairs are supremely comfortable.

Bars

Café Rose Red

MAP P.38, POCKET MAP C5
Cordoeaniersstraat 16 ☎ 050 33 90 51, ⓦ cordoeanier.be/en/rosered.php. Daily except Tues 11am–11.30pm.
Intimate little lounge bar with red banquettes located a couple of minutes' walk north of the Burg, where there's an excellent range of beers with seven on draught. The bar specializes in Trappist beers, selling – and this is very unusual – bottled beers from all six of Belgium's Trappist breweries: Achel, Chimay, Orval, Rochefort, Westmalle and Westvleteren. The

De Garre

bar is in an ancient building – hence the beamed ceiling – and there's a tiny courtyard out back.

Est Wijnbar

MAP P.38, POCKET MAP D6
Braambergstraat 7 ☎ 0478 45 05 55, ⓦ www.wijnbarest.be. Fri to Mon 4pm to midnight; closed Tues–Thurs.
A lively little wine bar, with a friendly and relaxed atmosphere, an extensive cellar and more than twenty wines available by the glass every day. It's especially strong on New World vintages. There's live (and free) jazz, blues and folk music every Sun from 8pm; the premises are small, so expect a crush.

De Garre

MAP P.38, POCKET MAP C6
De Garre 1. ☎ 050 34 10 29, ⓦ degarre.be. Mon-Fri & Sun noon–midnight, Sat 11am–12.30am.
Down a narrow alley off Breidelstraat, in between the Markt and the Burg, this cramped but charming and very ancient tavern (*estaminet*) has an outstanding range of Belgian beers and tasty snacks, while classical music adds to the relaxing air.

South of the Markt

The busy and bustling area to the south of the Markt holds several of the city's key buildings and leading museums. The area is at its prettiest among the old lanes and alleys near the cathedral, St-Salvatorskathedraal, which lays claim to be the city's most satisfying church, though the nearby Onze Lieve Vrouwekerk comes a close second. There is more cutesiness in the huddle of whitewashed cottages of the Begijnhof and at the adjacent Minnewater, the so-called "Lake of Love", a pleasant preamble to the ramparts beyond. As for the museums, St-Janshospitaal offers the exquisite medieval paintings of Hans Memling; the Gruuthuse is strong on applied art, especially tapestries and antique furniture, though it's currently closed for refurbishment; and the Groeninge Museum holds a simply wonderful, world-beating sample of early Flemish art.

Arentshuis

MAP P.48, POCKET MAP C6.
Dijver 16 ☎ 050 44 87 43, ⓦ visitbruges.be.
Tues–Sun 9.30am–5pm. €6

The **Arentshuis** occupies a good-looking eighteenth-century mansion with a stately porticoed

The Arentshuis

entrance. Now a museum, the interior is divided into two separate sections: the ground floor is given over to temporary exhibitions, usually of fine art, while the **Brangwyn Museum** upstairs displays the moody sketches, etchings, lithographs, studies and paintings of the much-travelled artist Sir Frank Brangwyn (1867–1956). Born in Bruges of Welsh parents, Brangwyn flitted between Britain and Belgium, donating this sample of his work to his native town in 1936. Apprenticed to William Morris in the early 1880s and an official UK war artist in World War I, Brangwyn was nothing if not versatile, turning his hand to several different media, though his forceful drawings and sketches are much more appealing than his paintings, which often slide into sentimentality. In the particular, look out for the sequence of line drawings exploring industrial themes – powerful, almost melodramatic scenes of shipbuilding and shipbreaking, docks, construction and the

The humpbacked St-Bonifaciusbrug

like. This penchant for dark and gloomy industrial scenes bore little relationship to the British artistic trends of his day and they attracted muted reviews. Better received were his murals, whose bold designs and strong colours attracted almost universal acclaim – and a 1920s commission to turn out a series for Britain's House of Lords. In the event, these murals, whose theme was the splendour of the British Empire, ended up in Swansea Guildhall, though two of the component parts – one sketch and one painting – are displayed here in the Arentshuis.

Arentspark

MAP P.48, POCKET MAP C6–C7.

The Arentshuis stands in the north corner of the pocket-sized **Arentspark**, whose brace of forlorn stone columns are all that remain of the Waterhalle, a large trading hall which once straddled the most central of the city's canals but was demolished in 1787 after the canal was covered over. Also in the Arentspark is the tiniest of humpbacked bridges

– **St-Bonifaciusbrug** – whose stonework is framed against a tumble of antique brick houses. One of Bruges's most picturesque (and photographed) spots, the bridge looks like the epitome of everything medieval, but in fact it was only built in 1910. It takes its name from an eighth-century Anglo-Saxon missionary who Christianised the Germans and was stabbed to death by the more -obdurate Frisians. Next to the far side of the bridge is a pensive, modern **statue** of Juan Luis Vives (1492–1540), a Spanish Jew and good friend of Erasmus, who moved to Bruges in the early sixteenth century to avoid persecution. It was a wise decision: back in Spain his family had converted to Christianity, but that failed to save them. His father was burnt at the stake in 1525 and his dead mother was dug up and her bones burned. Curiously, Vives also spent time at the court of Henry VIII, where his refusal to accept the legitimacy of the king's divorce from Catherine of Aragon cost him a stretch in prison.

Markets in Bruges

Bruges has a weekly food and flower market on the Markt (Wed 8am–1pm) and a more general food and clothes market on the Beursplein (Sat 8am–1pm). There's also a flea market along the Dijver and neighbouring Vismarkt (mid-March to mid-Nov Sat & Sun 10am–6pm), though there are more souvenir and craft stalls here than bric-à-brac places, and the tourist crowds mean that bargains are few and far between. If you're after a bargain, you might consider popping over to the much larger flea market in Ghent (see page 101).

Gruuthuse Museum

MAP P.48, POCKET MAP C7.
Dijver 17 ☏ 050 44 87 43, ⓌW visitbruges.be.
Closed for refurbishment until 2019.
The **Gruuthuse Museum** is located inside a rambling mansion that dates from the fifteenth century. The building is a fine example of civil Gothic – and neo-Gothic – architecture and it takes its name from the house owners' historical right to tax the

gruit, the dried herb and flower mixture once added to barley during the beer-brewing process to improve the flavour. The last lord of the Gruuthuse died in 1492 and a century later Philip II of Spain snaffled up the mansion, only for one of his successors to give it to a loyal follower, who installed a charity pawnbroker here – the so-called "Mount of Piety". In 1875, the city of Bruges bought what was, by then, a dilapidated

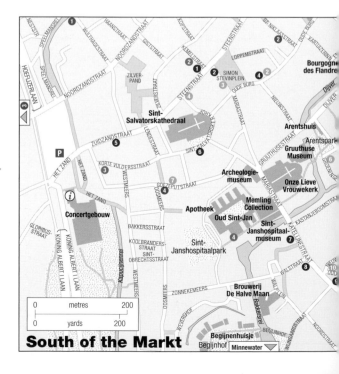

South of the Markt

ruin and commissioned Louis Delacenserie to revamp and restore the place. It was a good choice, as Delacenserie specialized in restorations, and today's exterior is a seamless blend of the late-medieval original and the neo-Gothic. Thereafter, the mansion was turned into a museum to hold a hotchpotch of Flemish fine, applied and decorative arts, mostly dating from the medieval and early modern period. The museum's strongest suit is its superb collection of **tapestries**, mostly woven in Brussels or Bruges during the sixteenth and seventeenth centuries (see page 62). The museum's most famous artefact is, however, a polychromatic terracotta bust of a youthful Emperor Charles V. The house's most unusual feature is the oak-panelled **oratory** that juts out from the first floor to overlook the altar of the Onze Lieve Vrouwekerk next

Gruuthuse Museum

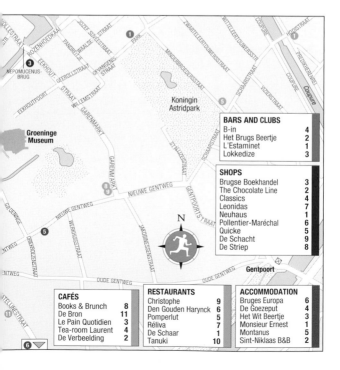

BARS AND CLUBS

B-in	4
Het Brugs Beertje	2
L'Estaminet	1
Lokkedize	3

SHOPS

Brugse Boekhandel	3
The Chocolate Line	2
Classics	4
Leonidas	7
Neuhaus	1
Pollentier-Maréchal	6
Quicke	5
De Schacht	9
De Striep	8

CAFÉS

Books & Brunch	8
De Bron	11
Le Pain Quotidien	3
Tea-room Laurent	4
De Verbeelding	2

RESTAURANTS

Christophe	9
Den Gouden Harynck	6
Pomperlut	5
Réliva	7
De Schaar	1
Tanuki	10

ACCOMMODATION

Bruges Europa	6
De Goezeput	4
Het Wit Beertje	3
Monsieur Ernest	1
Montanus	5
Sint-Niklaas B&B	2

Groeninge Museum

door (see page 54). The oratory allowed the lords of the *gruit* to worship without leaving home – a real social coup.

Groeninge Museum

MAP P.48, POCKET MAP D6–D7.
Dijver 12. ☎ 050 44 87 43, ⓦ visitbruges. be. Tues–Sun 9.30am–5pm. €12, including Arentshuis (see page 46).
Medieval Flanders was one of the most artistically productive parts of Europe, with each of the cloth towns, especially Bruges and Ghent, trying to outdo its rivals with the quality of its religious art. Today, the works of these early Flemish painters, known as the **Flemish Primitives**, are highly prized and an exquisite sample is displayed in the fifteen-room **Groeninge Museum** here in Bruges. **Jan van Eyck** is generally regarded as the first of the Flemish Primitives and has even been credited with the invention of oil painting itself – though it seems more likely that he simply perfected a new technique by thinning his paint with (the newly discovered) turpentine, thus making it more flexible. Van Eyck's most celebrated work is the *Adoration of the Mystic Lamb*, a stunningly beautiful altarpiece displayed in St-Baafskathedraal in Ghent (see page 94). The painting was revolutionary in its realism, for the first time using elements of native landscape in depicting biblical themes, and it is this finely observed realism that remains the hallmark of the Flemish Primitives and underpins a complex symbolism. Mostly the symbolism in the art from this period was religious, but sometimes it was secular, representing a distinct nod to the humanism that was gathering pace in Flanders.

The descriptions on page 52 detail some of the key works by four of the principal Flemish Primitives – **Jan van Eyck**, **Hugo van der Goes**, **Gerard David** and **Hieronymus Bosch**. There are also two fine and roughly contemporaneous copies of works by **Rogier van der Weyden** (1399–1464). The first is the tiny *Portrait of Philip the Good*, in which the pallor of the duke's aquiline features, along with the brightness of his hatpin and chain of office, are skilfully balanced by the sombre cloak and hat. The second and much larger painting, *St Luke painting the Portrait of Our Lady*, is a rendering of a popular if highly improbable legend claiming that Luke painted Mary – thereby becoming the patron saint of painters. One of van der Weyden's pupils was the talented **Hans Memling** (1430–94), who is well represented here by the splendid *Moreel Triptych* and has six works at the St-Janshospitaalmuseum (see page 57).

The Flemish Primitives are the Groeninge's star turn, but the museum also holds a substantial collection of later Belgian art. The collection of late sixteenth- and seventeenth-century paintings isn't especially strong, but there's enough to demonstrate the period's watering down of religious themes in favour of more secular preoccupations. In particular, **Pieter Pourbus** (1523–84) is seen at his best in a series of austere and often surprisingly unflattering portraits of the movers and shakers of his day. There's also his *Last Judgement*, a much larger but atypical work, crammed with muscular men and fleshy women. Completed in 1551, its inspiration came from Michelangelo's Sistine Chapel.

The museum also has a significant sample of nineteenth- and early twentieth-century Belgian art with the obvious highlight being the Expressionists, most memorably the work of the talented **Constant Permeke** (1886–1952). Wounded in World War I, Permeke's grim wartime experiences helped him to develop a distinctive style in which his subjects – usually agricultural workers, fishermen and so forth – were monumental in form, but invested with sombre, sometimes threatening emotion. His charcoal drawing *The Angelus* is a typically dark and earthy representation of Belgian peasant life dated

to 1934. In similar vein is the enormous *Last Supper* by **Gustave van de Woestijne** (1881–1947), in which Jesus and the disciples – all elliptical eyes and restrained movement – are trapped within prison-like walls.

Last but not least, the Groeninge has a small but choice selection of **Belgian Surrealists**, including a clutch of works by the inventive **Marcel Broodthaers** (1924–76), notably his tongue-in-cheek *Les Animaux de la Ferme*. There's also the spookily stark surrealism of *Serenity* by **Paul Delvaux** (1897–1994). One of the most interesting of Belgium's modern artists, Delvaux started out as an Expressionist but came to – and stayed with – Surrealism in the 1930s. Two of his pet motifs were train stations, in one guise or another, and nude or semi-nude women set against some sort of classical backdrop, all intended to usher the viewer into the unconscious. At their best, his paintings achieve an almost palpable sense of foreboding. This section also has a couple of minor oil paintings and several etchings and drawings by **James Ensor**

Flemish masterpieces at the Groeninge Museum

The Flemish Primitives at the Groeninge

Jan van Eyck (1385–1441)

Jan van Eyck lived and worked in Bruges from 1430 until his death eleven years later. The Groeninge has two gorgeous examples of his work, beginning with the miniature portrait of his wife, Margareta van Eyck, painted in 1439 and bearing his motto, "als ich can" (the best I can do). The painting is very much a private picture and one that had no commercial value, marking a step away from the sponsored art – and religious preoccupations – of previous Flemish artists. The second Eyck painting is the remarkable *Madonna and Child with Canon George van der Paele*, a glowing and richly symbolic work with three figures surrounding the Madonna and child: the kneeling canon, St George (his patron saint) and St Donatian, to whom he is being presented. St George doffs his helmet to salute the infant Christ and speaks by means of the Hebrew word "Adonai" (Lord) inscribed on his chin strap, while Jesus replies through the green parrot he holds: folklore asserted that this type of parrot was fond of saying "Ave", the Latin for "welcome" or "hail". Audaciously, Van Eyck has broken with religious tradition by painting the canon amongst the saints rather than as a lesser figure.

Hugo van der Goes (d.1482)

Hugo van der Goes is a shadowy figure, though it is known that he became master of the painters' guild in Ghent in 1467. Eight years later, he entered a Ghent priory as a lay brother, perhaps on account of the prolonged bouts of acute depression that afflicted him. Few of his paintings have survived, but his last work, the luminescent Death of Our Lady, is here at the Groeninge. Sticking to religious legend, the Apostles have been miraculously transported to Mary's deathbed, where, in a state of agitation, they surround the prostrate woman. Mary is dressed in blue, but there are no signs of luxury, reflecting both der Goes' asceticism and his polemic – the artist may well have been appalled by the church's love of glitter and gold.

Gerard David (c.1460–1523)

Born near Gouda, **Gerard David** moved to Bruges in his early twenties. Soon admitted into the local painters' guild, he quickly rose through the ranks, becoming the city's leading artistic light after the death of **Hans Memling** (see page 58). Official commissions rained in on David, mostly for religious paintings, which he approached in a formal manner but with a fine eye for detail. The Groeninge holds two delightful examples of his work, starting with the *Baptism of Christ* triptych, in which, in the central panel, a boyish, lightly bearded Christ is depicted as part of the Holy Trinity. There's also one of David's few secular ventures in the Groeninge, the intriguing *Judgement of Cambyses*, painted on two oak panels. Based on a Persian legend related by Herodotus, the first panel's background shows the corrupt judge Sisamnes accepting a bribe, with his subsequent arrest by grim-faced aldermen filling the foreground. The aldermen crowd in on Sisamnes and, as the king sentences him to be flayed alive, fear sweeps over the judge's face. In the gruesome second panel the king's servants carry out the judgement, while behind, in the top-right corner, the fable is completed with the judge's son dispensing justice from his father's old chair, which is now draped with the flayed skin.

Hieronymus Bosch (1450-1516)

The work of **Hieronymus Bosch** excels in its detail, but the subject matter was very different with his Last Judgement comprising a trio of oak panels crammed with mysterious beasts, microscopic mutants and scenes of awful cruelty – men boiled in a pit or cut in half by a giant knife. It looks like unbridled fantasy, but in fact the scenes were read as symbols, a veritable strip cartoon of legend, proverb and tradition. Indeed Bosch's religious orthodoxy is confirmed by the appeal his work had for that most Catholic of Spanish kings, Philip II.

(1860–1949), one of Belgium's most innovative painters, and **Magritte**'s (1898–1967) characteristically unnerving *The Assault*.

Most of the individual paintings mentioned should be on display, but the collection is regularly rotated; be sure to pick up a floor plan at reception.

Onze Lieve Vrouwekerk

MAP P.48, POCKET MAP C7.
Mariastraat ⊕ 050 44 87 43, ⓌⓌ visitbruges. be. Mon–Sat 9.30am–5pm, Sun 1.30–5pm. Free, but chancel €6.

The **Onze Lieve Vrouwekerk** (Church of Our Lady) is a rambling shambles of a building, a clamour of different dates and styles whose brick spire is – at 115.5m – the highest brick tower in Belgium. The **nave** was three hundred years in the making, an architecturally discordant affair, whose thirteenth-century grey-stone central aisle is the oldest part of the church. The central aisle blends in with the south aisle, but the later, fourteenth-century north aisle doesn't mesh at all – even the columns aren't aligned. This was the result of changing fashions,

not slapdash work: the high Gothic north aisle was intended to be the start of a complete remodelling of the church, but the money ran out before the project was finished. In the south aisle is the church's most acclaimed objet d'art, a delicate marble *Madonna and Child* by **Michelangelo**. Purchased by a Bruges merchant, this was the only one of Michelangelo's works to leave Italy during the artist's lifetime and it had a significant influence on painters working in Bruges at the time, though its present setting – beneath gloomy stone walls and set within a gaudy Baroque altar – is hardly prepossessing.

The most diverting part of the **Onze Lieve Vrouwekerk** is the **chancel**, which lies beyond the heavy-duty black-and-white marble rood screen. Here, you'll find the **mausoleums** of Charles the Bold and his daughter Mary of Burgundy (see page 55), two exquisite examples of Renaissance artistry, their side panels decorated with coats of arms connected by the most intricate of floral designs. The royal figures are enhanced in the detail,

Onze Lieve Vrouwekerk

The earthly remains of Mary of Burgundy and Charles the Bold

The last independent rulers of Flanders were Charles the Bold, the **Duke of Burgundy**, and his daughter **Mary of Burgundy**, both of whom died in unfortunate circumstances: Charles during the siege of the French city of Nancy in 1477 and Mary after a riding accident in 1482. Mary's death was a real surprise, but not so her father's – Charles was always fighting someone. Mary was married to **Maximillian**, a Habsburg prince and future Holy Roman Emperor, who inherited her territories on her death – thus, at a dynastic stroke, Flanders was incorporated into the Habsburg empire with all the dreadful consequences that would entail.

In the sixteenth century, the Habsburgs relocated to Spain, but they were keen to emphasize their connections with, and historical authority over, Flanders. Nothing did this quite as well as the ceremonial burial – or reburial – of bits of royal body. Mary was safely ensconced in Bruges's Onze Lieve Vrouwekerk, but the body of Charles was in a makeshift grave in Nancy. The Emperor Charles V, the great grandson of Charles the Bold, had this body exhumed and carried to Bruges, where it was reinterred next to Mary. Or at least he thought he had: there were persistent rumours that the French – the traditional enemies of the Habsburgs – had deliberately handed over a dud skeleton. In the 1970s, archeologists had a bash at solving the mystery by digging beneath Charles and Mary's mausoleums in the Onze Lieve Vrouwekerk, but among the assorted tombs, they failed to authoritatively identify either the body or even the tomb of Charles. Things ran more smoothly in Mary's case, however, with her skeleton confirming the known details of her hunting accident. Moreover, buried alongside her was the **urn** which contained the heart of her son, Philip the Fair, placed here in 1506. More archeological harrumphing over the remains of poor old Charles is likely at some point or another.

from the helmet and gauntlets placed gracefully by Charles' side to the pair of watchful dogs nestled at Mary's feet. Curiously, the **hole** dug by archeologists beneath the mausoleums during the 1970s to discover who was actually buried here was never filled in, so you can see the burial vaults of several unknown medieval dignitaries, though three of them have been moved across to the Lanchals Chapel (see below). The coats of arms above the choir stalls are those of the knights of the Order of the Golden Fleece (see page 61), who met here in 1468.

In the ambulatory, across from the mausoleums, the **Lanchals Chapel** holds the imposing Baroque gravestone of Pieter Lanchals, a one-time Habsburg official who had his head lopped off by the citizens of Bruges in 1488. Legend asserts that he was beheaded for his opposition to Maximilian's temporary imprisonment in the Craenenburg (see page 30) and that, to atone for the crime, Bruges was later obliged to introduce swans onto its canals. Both tales are, however, later fabrications: Lanchals actually had his head lopped off for being

Coat of arms above the entrance to St-Janshospitaal

corrupt and was soon forgotten by his erstwhile sponsor, while the swan story originated with the swan that adorns his gravestone – the bird was the man's emblem, appropriately enough, as his name means "long neck". In front of the Lanchals gravestone are the three relocated **medieval burial vaults** moved across from beneath the royal mausoleums. Each is plastered with lime mortar and the inside walls sport brightly coloured **grave frescoes**, a type of art which flourished hereabouts in late medieval times. The iconography is fairly consistent, with the long sides mostly bearing one, sometimes two, angels apiece, and most of the angels are shown swinging thuribles (the vessels in which incense is burnt during religious ceremonies). Typically, the short sides show the Crucifixion and a Virgin and Child. The background decoration is more varied, with crosses, stars and dots all making appearances as well as two main sorts of flower – roses and bluebells. The frescoes were painted freehand and executed at great speed – Flemings were then buried on the day they died –

hence the delightful immediacy of the work.

St-Janshospitaal

MAP P.48, POCKET MAP C7.
Mariastraat 38 ⓘ 050 44 87 43,
ⓦ visitbruges.be. Apotheek (Apothecary):
Tues–Sun 9.30am–12.30pm &
1.30–5pm. Entry to Apotheek free with St-
Janshospitaalmuseum ticket (see p.57).

A sprawling complex, **St-Janshospitaal** sheltered the sick of mind and body from medieval times until well into the nineteenth century. The oldest part – at the front on Mariastraat, behind two church-like gable ends – has been turned into the excellent **St-Janshospitaalmuseum** (see p.57), whilst the nineteenth-century annexe, reached along a narrow passageway on the north side of the museum, has been converted into a really rather mundane events and exhibition centre called – rather confusingly – **Oud St-Jan**. As you stroll down the passageway, you pass the old **Apotheek**, where one room holds dozens of ex-votos, the other an ancient dispensing counter flanked by a brigade of vintage apothecary's jars.

St-Janshospitaalmuseum

MAP P.48, POCKET MAP C7.
Mariastraat 38 ☏ 050 44 87 43, ⓦ visit
bruges.be. Tues–Sun 9.30am–5pm. €12.

At the front of the St-Janshospitaal complex, the **St-Janshospitaalmuseum** occupies three distinct spaces – the old, stone-arched hospital ward, the adjoining chapel and a modern floor inserted above. The hospital ward and the floor above are often used for temporary exhibitions, which means that the museum's collection of artefacts on the hospital itself – including a pair of sedan chairs used to carry the infirm to the hospital in emergencies and a set of photos of nuns in their fanciful habits – can be shunted around or even removed. The chapel and its immediate environs, on the other hand, always feature several key works by **Hans Memling** (see page 58) plus a number of other paintings and objets d'art. Highlights include an exquisite *Deposition of Christ*, a late fifteenth-century version of an original by **Rogier van der Weyden**, and a stylish, intimately observed diptych by **Jan Provoost** with portraits of Christ and the donor (a friar) on the front and a skull on the back – the skull a reminder of the donor's mortality. There's also Jan Beerblock's *The Wards of St Janshospitaal*, a minutely detailed painting of the hospital ward as it was in the late-eighteenth century, the patients tucked away in row upon row of tiny, cupboard-like beds. There were 150 beds in total divided into three sections: one for women, one for men and the third for the dying. The nuns had a fine reputation for the quality of their ministrations, but presumably being moved to the dying beds was something of a disappointment – though none of the patients have left any records.

St-Salvatorskathedraal

MAP P.48, POCKET MAP B6–C6
Steenstraat ☏ 050 33 61 88,
ⓦ sintsalvator.be. Mon–Fri 10am–1pm &
2–5.30pm, Sat 10am–1pm & 2–3.30pm,
Sun 11.30am–noon & 2–5pm. Free.

Rising high above its surroundings, **St-Salvatorskathedraal** (Holy Saviour Cathedral) is a largely Gothic edifice that mostly dates

SOUTH OF THE MARKT

View of St-Salvatorskathedraal and the rooftops of Bruges

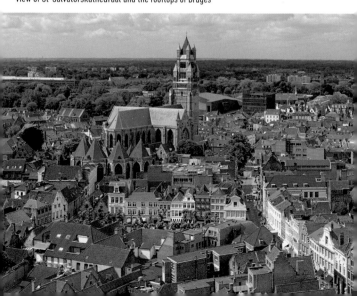

The Memling Collection

St-Janshospitaalmuseum holds six wonderful works by **Hans Memling** (1433–94). Born near Frankfurt, Memling spent most of his working life in Bruges, where Rogier van der Weyden tutored him. He adopted much of his mentor's style and stuck to the detailed symbolism of his contemporaries, but his painterly manner was distinctly restrained, often pious and grave. Graceful and warmly coloured, his figures also had a velvet-like quality that greatly appealed to the city's burghers, whose enthusiasm made Memling a rich man – in 1480 he was listed among the town's major moneylenders.

Of the Memling works on display, the most unusual is the **Reliquary of St Ursula**, comprising a miniature wooden Gothic church painted with the story of St Ursula. Memling condensed the legend into six panels beginning with Ursula and her ten companions landing at Cologne and Basle before reaching Rome at the end of their pilgrimage. Things go badly wrong on the way back: they leave Basle in good order but are then – in the last two panels – massacred by Huns as they pass through Germany. Memling had a religious point to make, but today it's the mass of incidental detail that makes the reliquary so enchanting, providing an intriguing evocation of the late medieval world. Close by are two **triptychs**, a *Lamentation* and an *Adoration of the Magi*, in which there's a gentle nervousness in the approach of the Magi, here shown as the kings of Spain, Arabia and Ethiopia.

The middle panel of Memling's **St John Altarpiece** displays the exquisite Marriage of St Catherine in which the saint, who represents contemplation, is shown receiving a ring from the baby Jesus to seal their spiritual union. Catherine was one of the most popular of medieval saints, not least because although she was martyred in the fourth century, her body was reportedly rediscovered on Mount

Sinai several centuries later with a stream of healing oil issuing from her body. Behind Jesus to the left stands St John and behind him, if you look closely, is the giant wooden crane that once dominated the Kraanplein (see page 71). The side panels depict the beheading of St John the Baptist and a visionary St John writing the Book of Revelation on the bare and rocky island of Patmos. Once again, it's the detail that impresses: between the inner and outer rainbows above St John, for instance, the prophets play music on tiny instruments, including a lute, a flute, a harp and a hurdy-gurdy.

In a side-chapel adjoining the main chapel is Memling's **Virgin**

and Martin van Nieuwenhove, a diptych depicting the eponymous merchant in the full flush of youth and with a hint of arrogance: his lips pout, his hair cascades down to his shoulders and he is dressed in the most fashionable of doublets – by the middle of the 1480s, when the portrait was commissioned, no Bruges merchant wanted to appear too pious. Opposite, the Virgin gets the full stereotypical treatment from the oval face and the almond-shaped eyes through to full cheeks, thin nose and bunched lower lip.

Also in the side chapel, Memling's skill as a portraitist is demonstrated to exquisite effect in his **Portrait of a Young Woman**, where the richly dressed subject stares dreamily into the middle distance, her hands – in a superb optical illusion – seeming to clasp the picture frame. The lighting is subtle and sensuous, with the woman set against a dark background, her gauze veil dappling the side of her face. A high forehead was then considered a sign of great womanly beauty, so her hair is pulled right back and was probably plucked, as are her eyebrows. There's no knowing who the woman was, but in the seventeenth century her fancy headgear convinced observers that she was one of the legendary Persian sibyls who predicted Christ's birth; they added the cartouche in the top left-hand corner, describing her as Sibylla Sambetha and the painting is often referred to by this name.

from the late-thirteenth century, though the Flamboyant Gothic ambulatory was added some two centuries later. A parish church for most of its history, it was only made a cathedral in 1834 following the destruction of St Donatian's (see page 42) by the French. This change of status prompted ecclesiastical rumblings – nearby Onze Lieve Vrouwekerk (see page 54) was bigger and its spire higher – and when part of St Salvator's went up in smoke in 1839, the opportunity was taken to make its tower higher and grander in a romantic rendition of the Romanesque style.

Slowly emerging from a seemingly interminable restoration, the cathedral's **nave** remains a cheerless, cavernous affair despite lashings of new paint. The star turn is the **set of eight paintings** by Jan van Orley displayed in the transepts. Commissioned in the 1730s, the paintings were used for the manufacture of a matching set of **tapestries** from a Brussels workshop and, remarkably enough, these have survived too and hang in sequence in the choir and nave.

Each of the eight scenes features a familiar episode from the life of Christ, complete with a handful of animals, including a remarkably determined Palm Sunday donkey. The tapestries are actually mirror images of the paintings as the weavers worked with the rear of the tapestries uppermost on their looms; the weavers also had sight of the tapestry paintings, as the originals were too valuable to be kept beside the looms. Also in the choir are the painted escutcheons of the members of the **Order of the Golden Fleece**, which met here in 1478 (see page 61). Adjoining the nave, in the floor of the **porch** behind the old main doors, look out also for the recently excavated tombs, whose interior walls are decorated with grave frescoes that follow the same design as those in the Lanchals Chapel (see page 55).

Entered from the cathedral nave, the **Treasury** (Schatkamer; Mon–Fri & Sun 2–5pm; free) occupies the neo-Gothic chapterhouse, whose cloistered rooms are packed with ecclesiastical tackle, from religious paintings and statues

Interior of St-Salvatorskathedraal

through to an assortment of reliquaries, vestments and croziers. The labelling is only average, so it's a good idea to pick up the English-language mini-guide at the entrance. The treasury's finest painting is a gruesome, oak-panel triptych, *The Martyrdom of St Hippolytus*, by **Dieric Bouts** (1410–75), who was probably born in Leuven, and **Hugo van der Goes** (d. 1482), from Ghent. The right panel depicts the Roman Emperor Decius, a notorious persecutor of Christians, trying to persuade the priest Hippolytus to abjure his faith. He fails, and in the

The Martyrdom of St Hippolytus

Keeping your friends and enemies close: the Order of the Golden Fleece

Philip the Good, the Duke of Burgundy, invented the **Order of the Golden Fleece** in 1430 on the occasion of his marriage to Isabella of Portugal. Duke since 1419, Philip had spent much of his time curbing the power of the Flemish cities – including Bruges – but he was too economically dependent on them to feel entirely secure. To bolster his position, the duke was always on the lookout for ways to add lustre to his dynasty, hence his creation of the Order of the Golden Fleece, an exclusive, knightly club that harked back to the (supposed) age of chivalry. The choice of the name was a nod both to the wool weavers of Flanders, who provided him with most of his money, and to the legends of classical Greece. In the Greek story, a winged ram named Chrysomallus – gifted with the power of speech and a golden fleece – saved the life of Phrixus, presented him with his fleece and then flew off to become the constellation of Aries; it was this same fleece that Jason and the Argonauts later sought to recover. The Order's emblem was a golden ram.

Philip stipulated that **membership** of the Order be restricted to "noblemen in name and proven in valour...born and raised in legitimate wedlock". He promptly picked the **membership** and appointed himself Grand Master. It was a bit of a con trick, but it went down a treat and the 24 knights who were offered membership duly turned up at the first meeting in Lille in 1431. Thereafter, the Order met fairly regularly, gathering together for some mutual back-slapping, feasting and exchanging of presents. Bruges and Ghent were two favourite venues, and the Order met three times in the former: at St Donatian's Cathedral in 1431, at the Onze Lieve Vrouwekerk in 1468, and at St-Salvatorskathedraal in 1478. However, when the Habsburgs swallowed up Burgundy in the late-fifteenth century, the Order was rendered obsolete and the title "Grand Master" became just one of the family's many dynastic baubles.

Stained glass in St-Salvatorskathedraal

central panel Hippolytus is pulled to pieces by four horses. One other highlight here is the coin-like tokens the church wardens once gave to the poor. Each is inscribed with an entitlement – "W.B.", for instance, means bread for a week.

Archeologiemuseum

Map p.48, Pocket map C7.
Mariastraat 36 ☏ 050 44 87 43,
🌐 visitbruges.be. Tues–Sun 9.30am–
12.30pm & 1.30–5pm. €4.

An intricate skill: tapestry making in Bruges

Tapestry manufacture in Bruges began in the middle of the fourteenth century when the city was experiencing something of a boom. This embryonic industry soon came to be based on a dual system of workshop and outworker, the one using paid employees, the other with workers paid on a piecework basis. From the beginning, the town authorities took a keen interest in the business, ensuring consistency by a rigorous system of quality control. The other side of this interventionist policy was less palatable: wages were kept down and the workers were hardly ever able to accumulate enough capital to buy either their own looms or even the raw materials, thereby ensuring the burghers were in tight control.

There were two great periods of **Bruges tapestry-making**, the first from the early fifteenth until the middle of the sixteenth century, the second from the 1580s to the 1790s. Tapestry production was a cross between **embroidery and ordinary weaving**. It consisted of interlacing a wool weft above and below the strings of a vertical linen "chain", a process similar to weaving. However, the weaver had to stop to change colour, requiring as many shuttles for the weft as he or she had colours, as in embroidery. The appearance of a tapestry was entirely determined by the weft, the design being taken from a painting – or cartoon of a painting – to which the weaver made constant reference. Standard-size tapestries took six months to make and were produced exclusively for the very wealthy. The most famous artists of the day were often involved in the preparatory paintings – amongst many, Pieter Paul Rubens, Bernard van Orley and David Teniers all had tapestry commissions.

There were only two significant **types of tapestry**: decorative, principally verdures, showing scenes of foliage in an almost abstract way; and pictorial (the Bruges speciality) – usually variations on the same basic themes, particularly rural life, knights, hunting parties, classical gods and goddesses and religious scenes. Over the centuries, changes in style were strictly limited, though the early part of the seventeenth century saw an increased use of elaborate woven borders, an appreciation of perspective and the use of a far brighter, more varied range of colours.

Given the city's pride in its past, you would expect the **Archeologiemuseum** (Archeological Museum) to be an impressive affair crammed with exhibits, but it's a particularly modest affair. The most interesting section is devoted to the city's medieval tanners, featuring an assortment of decrepit leather shoes recovered from various digs.

Brouwerij De Halve Maan

MAP P.48, POCKET MAP C7
Walplein 26 ☎ 050 44 42 22,
ⓦ halvemaan.be. 45min guided tours daily 11am–4pm, 5pm on Saturday. €9

Beside a pleasant square, the long-established **Brouwerij De Halve Maan** (Half Moon Brewery) offers frequent guided tours of its premises, which include a glass of the brewery's most popular beer, Brugse Zot. There is a café-bar and a beer shop here too. Interestingly, the brewery recently crowd-funded a 3km-long tunnel to take beer from the brewery here on Walplein to its bottling plant – and hey presto, no more brewery delivery vans.

Bottling at the Brouwerij De Halve Maan

Begijnhof

MAP P.48, POCKET MAP C8
Begijnhof ☎ 050 33 00 11,
ⓦ visitbruges.be. Daily 6.30am–6.30pm. Free.

Most tourists in Bruges zero in on the **Begijnhof**, just south of the centre, where a rough circle of old and infinitely pretty whitewashed houses surrounds a central green, which looks a treat in spring, when a carpet of daffodils pushes up between the wind-bent elms. There were once *begijnhoven* all over Belgium, and this is one of the few to have survived in good nick. They date back to the twelfth century, when a Liège priest – a certain Lambert le Bègue – encouraged widows and unmarried women to live in communities, the better to do pious acts, especially caring for the sick. These communities were different from convents in so far as the inhabitants – the **beguines** (*begijnen*) – did not have to take conventual vows and had the right to return to the secular world if they wished. Margaret, Countess of Flanders, founded Bruges'

The Minnewater or "Lake of Love"

begijnhof in 1245, and although most of the houses now standing date from the eighteenth century, the medieval layout has survived intact, preserving the impression of the *begijnhof* as a self-contained village, with access controlled through two large and particularly handsome gates. The houses are still in private hands but, with the Beguines long gone, they're now occupied by a mixture of single, elderly women and Benedictine nuns, whom you'll sometimes see flitting around in their habits, mostly on their way to and from the **Begijnhofkerk**, a surprisingly large church with a set of gaudy altarpieces. Only one house in the *begijnhof* is open to the public – the **Begijnenhuisje** (Begijnhof 24; daily 10am–5pm; €2), a small-scale celebration of the simple life of the beguines, comprising a couple of living rooms and a mini-cloister. The prime exhibit is the *schapraai*, a traditional beguine's cupboard, which was a frugal combination of dining table, cutlery cabinet and larder.

Minnewater

MAP P.48, POCKET MAP C8

Facing the more southerly of the *begijnhof*'s two gates is the **Minnewater**, often hyped as the city's "Lake of Love". The tag certainly gets the canoodlers going, but in fact the lake – more a large pond – started life as a city harbour. The distinctive stone **lock house** at the head of the Minnewater recalls its earlier function, though it's actually a very fanciful nineteenth-century reconstruction of the medieval original. The **Poertoren**, on the west bank at the far end of the lake, is more authentic, its brown brickwork dating from 1398 and once forming part of the city wall. This is where the city kept its gunpowder – hence the name, "powder tower". Beside the Poertoren, a footbridge spans the southern end of the Minnewater to reach the leafy expanse of **Minnewaterpark**, which trails north back towards Wijngaardstraat, or you can keep on going along the wooded footpath that threads its way along the former city **ramparts**.

Shops

Brugse Boekhandel

MAP P.48, POCKET MAP D6
Dijver 2 ☎ 050 33 29 52,
ⓦ brugseboekhandel.be. Mon–Sat
9am–12.30pm & 1.30–6.30pm.
Family-owned, the long-established
Brugse Boekhandel is an amiable
general bookstore that is especially
good for books about Bruges, both
past and present, including tourist
guides. Also does a competent
side-line in English language
novels, has a better than average
selection of postcards, sells English-
language newspapers and stocks
an outstanding range of books on
local lace.

The Chocolate Line

MAP P.48, POCKET MAP C6
Simon Stevinplein 19 ☎ 050 34 10 90,
ⓦ thechocolateline.be. Mon & Sun
10.30am–6.30pm, Tues–Sat 9.30am–
6.30pm
The best chocolate shop in
town – and there's some serious
competition – with everything
handmade using natural
ingredients. Truffles and pralines
are two specialities and the
chocolates come in all sorts of
tempting shapes and sizes. Boxes of
mixed chocolates are sold in various
quantities: a 250g box costs €18.

Classics

MAP P.48, POCKET MAP C6
Oude Burg 32 ☎ 050 33 90 58, ⓦ classics-
brugge.be. Tues–Sat 10am–noon & 2–6pm.
In business since the 1970s, this
cosy family-owned art shop is
a mixed bag of a place, selling
everything from fine art, tapestries,
furniture and antiques to more
modern objects in traditional styles.
Also stocks Indian textiles and is
good for handmade jewellery.

Leonidas

MAP P.48, POCKET MAP C7
Katelijnestraat 24 ☎ 050 34 69 41,
ⓦ leonidas.com. Daily 10am–6pm.
Leonidas is one of the biggest
chocolate-shop chains in
Belgium and has six outlets in
Bruges, including one here on
Katelijnestraat and another at the
train station. This particular branch
offers a wide selection of pralines
and candy confectionery all at very
competitive prices (around €10 for
250g), though their products are
more sugary than those of their
more exclusive/expensive rivals.
As with all chocolate shops along
Katelijnestraat, expect queues in
the summer.

Neuhaus

MAP P.48, POCKET MAP C6
Steenstraat 66 ☎ 050 33 15 30,
ⓦ neuhaus.be. Mon noon–6pm, Tues–Sat
10am–6pm, Sun 1–6pm.
Neuhaus is probably Belgium's
best chocolate chain and they sell
delicious and beautifully presented
chocolates. Check out their
specialities, such as the handmade
Caprices – pralines stuffed with
crispy nougat, fresh cream and
soft-centred chocolate – and the
delicious Manons – stuffed white
chocolates, which come with fresh
cream, vanilla and coffee fillings.

Neuhaus

There are two stores in Bruges; this outlet is the less crowded. €18 for a 250g box.

Pollentier-Maréchal

MAP P.48, POCKET MAP C7
St-Salvatorskerkhof 8 ☎ 050 33 18 04,
ⓦ pollentier-marechal.be. Tues–Fri 2–6pm,
Sat 10am–noon & 2–6pm.

Tucked up against St-Salvatorskathedraal, this antiquarian hideaway specializes in old and contemporary graphics and prints. They restore old paintings and engravings too and offer a top-quality framing service. Seascapes, hunting scenes and Bruges cityscapes predominate.

Quicke

MAP P.48, POCKET MAP B6
Zuidzandstraat 23 ☎ 050 33 23 00,
ⓦ quicke.be. Mon–Sat 10am–6.30pm.

The top shoe shop in Bruges, Quicke showcases the prime European seasonal collections, featuring the likes of Prada, Church's and Miu Miu. No surprise, then, that their shoes are expensive. It also sells a wide-range of less well-known brands

– for instance Santoni, Hogan and Bambu.

De Schacht

MAP P.48, POCKET MAP C7
Katelijnestraat 49 ☎ 050 33 44 24,
ⓦ de-schacht.be. Mon–Fri 9am–1pm & 1.30–6pm, Sat 10am–6pm.

Smart little shop whose speciality is paint materials for the artist – or at least budding artist. Also sells a good range of arty postcards, stationery and pens, both modern and traditional, including fountain pens and ink.

De Striep

MAP P.48, POCKET MAP C7
Katelijnestraat 42 ☎ 050 33 71 12,
ⓦ striepclub.be. Mon 1.30–7pm, Tues–Sat 9am–12.30pm & 1.30–7pm, plus first Sun in the month 2–6pm.

Comics are a Belgian speciality (remember Tintin), but this is the only comic-strip specialist in Bruges, stocking everything from run-of-the-mill cheapies to collector items in Flemish, French and even English. Stocks both new and second-hand comics as well as a scattering of hang-on-the-wall comic prints.

De Schacht

Cafés

Books & Brunch

MAP P.48, POCKET MAP D7
Garenmarkt 30 ① 050 70 90 79,
Ⓦ booksandbrunch.be. Mon–Fri 9am–3pm,
but closed during some school holidays.
There's a cosy, family vibe at
this cheerful little café, where
they do tasty, healthy lunches
and light meals prepared from
organic sources. Cakes too – try
the cupcakes – and a tasty cup of
coffee. Very child-friendly.

De Bron

MAP P.48, POCKET MAP D8
Katelijnestraat 82 ① 050 33 45 26, Ⓦ eethuis
debron.be. Mon–Fri 11.45am–2pm.
Many of the city's cafés and
restaurants offer vegetarian dishes,
but this pleasant little place is the
only exclusively vegetarian spot
per se, offering fresh, organic
food – lentil salad, stewed cabbage,
pumpkin, pickled radish and such
like. There is one main dish of the
day, which comes in three sizes –
small, medium and large (medium
is enough for most). A meal costs a
very reasonable €15–20. Cash only.

Le Pain Quotidien

MAP P.48, POCKET MAP C6
Simon Stevinplein 15 ① 050 34 29 21,
Ⓦ lepainquotidien.be. Mon–Sat 7am–7pm,
Sun 8am–6pm.
This popular café, part of a chain,
occupies a grand old building on
one of the city's busiest squares
and has a large terrace at the back.
Much of the success of the chain
is built upon its bread, wholefood
and baked every which way. A
substantial menu clocks up the
likes of salads, light bites and cakes
and they also do an excellent home-
made soup and bread (€6.90),
which makes a meal in itself.

Tea-room Laurent

MAP P.48, POCKET MAP C6
Steenstraat 79 ① 050 33 94 67,
Ⓦ newlaurent.com. Daily 9.30am–7.30pm.

Books & Brunch

No points for decor or atmosphere,
but the competitive prices at this
busy café attract locals by the score.
The snacks and light meals are
filling, if hardly finessed, but the
pancakes are delicious and begin at
a very reasonable €4. Located just
metres from the cathedral.

De Verbeelding

MAP P.48, POCKET MAP C6
Oude Burg 26 ① 050 33 82 94. Tues–Sat
noon–9pm.
This amenable, family-run café-
restaurant occupies notably cosy
premises in a handy location. Few
would say the food was brilliant,
but it is relatively inexpensive
(mains from around €12) and the
simpler dishes – meatballs for one –
are both filling and tasty.

Restaurants

Christophe

MAP P.48, POCKET MAP D7
Garenmarkt 34 ① 050 34 48 92,
Ⓦ christophe-brugge.be. Mon & Thurs–Sun
6–11pm.
Rural chic furnishings and fittings
make for a relaxing atmosphere at
this pocket–sized bistro, where a
Franco-Flemish menu is especially

Pomperlut

strong on meat. One exception is the excellent bouillabaisse. Daily specials are a feature and prices are competitive, with main courses averaging around €28.

Den Gouden Harynck

MAP P.48, POCKET MAP C7
Groeninge 25 ☎ 050 33 76 37,
ⓦ goudenharynck.be. Tues–Fri noon–
1.30pm & 7–8.30pm & Sat 7–8.30pm.
In a handsomely restored, seventeenth-century mansion, this smart and formal restaurant is one of the city's premier spots – with prices to match. It's French cuisine at its most polished with amuse-bouche followed by the likes of lobster and coquilles with cauliflower. A set-menu dinner costs €65–80, €45 at lunch times. Reservations essential.

Pomperlut

MAP P.48, POCKET MAP E6
Minderbroedersstraat 26 ☎ 050 70 86
26, ⓦ pomperlut.be. Wed & Sun 6–10pm,
Thurs–Sat noon–2pm & 6–10pm.
This first-rate restaurant has got most things dead right – from the ersatz medievalism of the decor (the house is old, but the wooden beams

and chimneypiece were inserted during the refurbishment) through to the Franco-Flemish cuisine. Try, for example, the vol au vent with quail breast and sweetbread. Mains average a fairly reasonable €31. Reservations essential.

Réliva

MAP P.48, POCKET MAP B7
Goezeputstraat 6 ☎ 050 33 13 07, ⓦ reliva.
be. Mon & Thurs 6–10pm, Fri–Sun
noon–2pm & 6–10pm.
This chic and relaxed restaurant may not quite deserve all its rave reviews, but there's no denying the inventive, carefully constructed menu and the pride they take in using organic ingredients. A sample dish is wild duck with celeriac cream with a port jus – indeed the sauces are truly delicious. Note, however, that they won't serve tap water. Mains average €30, less at lunch times. Reservations essential.

De Schaar

MAP P.48, POCKET MAP E6
Hooistraat 2 ☎ 050 33 59 79,
ⓦ bistrodeschaar.be. Daily except Wed &
Thurs noon–2pm & 6–9pm.
In the cosiest of terrace houses, complete with stepped gable, this appealing restaurant sits prettily beside the Coupure canal about ten minutes' walk southeast of the Burg. The speciality here is grilled meat – for example rack of lamb with wok vegetables and mustard sauce (€27) – but there are other gastronomic delights too, for instance duck with a raspberry sauce (€22). All are nicely served and presented.

Tanuki

MAP P.48, POCKET MAP C7
Oude Gentweg 1 ☎ 050 34 75 12, ⓦ tanuki.
be. Wed–Sun noon–2pm & 6.30–9.30pm;
closed two weeks in Jan & July.
Probably the best Japanese restaurant in town and certainly, if you've been in Belgium a long time, a welcome break from the heaviness of Flemish cuisine. The

menu features all the usual Japanese favourites – noodles, sushi and sashimi. Mains average €35. They must be doing something right – Tanuki celebrates its twenty-fifth anniversary this year.

Bars and clubs

B-in

MAP P.48, POCKET MAP C7
Oud St-Jan, off Mariastraat ☎ 050 31 13 00, ⓦ b-in.be. Tues–Sat 11am–3am, sometimes later. Free entry.
The coolest place in town, this slick bar, club and restaurant is kitted out in attractive modern style with low sofa-seats and an eye-grabbing mix of coloured fluorescent tubes and soft ceiling lights. Guest DJs play funky, uplifting house and the drinks and cocktails are reasonably priced. There's a canalside terrace too. The club gets going at about 11pm.

Het Brugs Beertje

MAP P.48, POCKET MAP C6
Kemelstraat 5 ☎ 050 33 96 16, ⓦ brugsbeertje.be. Mon & Thurs–Sun 4pm–midnight.
This small and friendly speciality beer bar – the "Little Bear" – claims a stock of three hundred brews (plus guest beers on draught), which aficionados reckon is one of the best selections in Belgium. It was opened by an enterprising local woman, Daisy Claeys, in the early 1980s, when she spotted an increasing interest in Belgian beers in general and speciality brews in particular. The bar is now very much on the tourist trail, attracting an international clientele. Simple food is served here too, including a cheese board with five types of cheese, paté and toasted sandwiches.

L'Estaminet

MAP P.48, POCKET MAP D6
Park 5 ☎ 050 33 09 16, ⓦ estaminet-brugge.be. Tues, Wed & Fri–Sun noon–1am or later, Thurs from 5pm–1am or later.

Groovy café-bar with a relaxed neighbourhood feel and (for Bruges) a diverse and cosmopolitan clientele. Drink either in the dark (and almost mysterious) interior or outside on the large sheltered terrace. The beer menu is well chosen, skilfully picking its way through Belgium's vast offering. One of the city's best hangouts, though the name of the place has seedy connotations: according to some local sources, *estaminet* is derived from the Spanish Habsburg garrison's search for women as in "*estan minetas*" – "Are there girls?"

Lokkedize

MAP P.48, POCKET MAP B7
Korte Vuldersstraat 33 ☎ 050 33 44 50, ⓦ bistrolokkedize.be. Daily except Tues 6pm–1am.
Attracting a youthful crowd, this sympathetic bar-cum-bistro – all subdued lighting, fresh flowers and bare brick walls – serves up a good line in Mediterranean (especially Greek) food, with main courses averaging around €11 and bar snacks from €7. There is regular live music too, everything from jazz and *chanson* through to R&B.

Het Brugs Beertje

North and east of the Markt

The gentle canals and mazy cobbled streets of northeast Bruges are extraordinarily pretty. In this uncrowded part of the centre, stretching out from Jan van Eyckplein to the old medieval moat, picturesque brick terraces, dating from the town's late medieval golden age, blend seamlessly with the grand Classical mansions of later years, all woven round a skein of black-blue canals. Northeast Bruges surprises the eye with its subtle variety, with everything from discreet shrines and miniature statues through to delightful neighbourhood churches, intimate arched doorways, handsome crow-step gables, bendy tiled roofs and scores of wonky-looking chimneys. The sheer prettiness of northeast Bruges is its main appeal, but nevertheless there are one or two obvious targets: a pair of Baroque churches – St-Annakerk and St-Walburgakerk – as well as the antique lace of the Kantcentrum (Lace Centre), and the Museum Onze-Lieve-Vrouw-ter-Potterie (Museum of Our Lady of the Pottery), which has an intriguing chapel and several fine Flemish tapestries.

St-Jakobskerk

MAP P.72, POCKET MAP B5
St-Jakobsplein ⊕ 050 44 87 43,
ⓦ visitbruges.be. April–Sept Mon–Sat
10am–noon & 2–5pm, Sun 2–5pm; Oct–
March daily 2–5pm. Free.

Religious painting in St-Jakobskerk

Not far from the Markt, the serious exterior of **St-Jakobskerk** (church of St James) mostly dates from the fifteenth century. In medieval times, the church was popular with foreign merchants, acting as a sort of prototype community centre. Inside, the church is mainly Baroque, its airy, triple-aisled **nave** interrupted and darkened by a grim marble rood screen with a cumbersome high altar lurking beyond. More appealing is the handsome Renaissance **burial chapel** of Ferry de Gros (d. 1547), to the right of the choir, which sports the elaborate, painted tomb of this well-to-do landowner. Unusually, the tomb has two shelves – on the top are the finely carved effigies of Ferry and his first wife, while below, on the lower shelf, is his second. Here also, above the chapel's altar, is an enamelled terracotta medallion of the Virgin

Monument to Jan van Eyck on Jan van Eyckplein square

and Child imported from Florence in the fifteenth century. No one knows quite how it ended up here, but there's no doubt that it influenced Flemish artists of the period. The walls of St-Jakobskerk are covered with around eighty **paintings**. They're not an especially distinguished bunch, but look out for the finely executed *Legend of St Lucy*, in St Anthony's Chapel – the first chapel on the left-hand side of the nave. A panel triptych by the Master of the St Lucy Legend, the painting illustrates the persecution of this fourth-century saint, who – legend has it – proved extremely difficult to dispose of: the men sent to arrest her found her immovable even with the assistance of a team of oxen (as in the third panel). In the next chapel along, look out also for the meditative *Madonna and the Seven Sorrows*, a triptych by **Pieter Pourbus** (1523–84), the leading local artist of his day.

Kraanplein

MAP P.72, POCKET MAP C5

Just off Vlamingstraat lies the **Kraanplein** – Crane Square – whose name recalls the enormous

wooden crane that once unloaded heavy goods from the adjoining river. Before it was covered over, the River Reie ran south from Jan van Eyckplein to the Markt, and the Kraanplein dock was one of the busiest parts of this central waterway. Mounted on a revolving post like a windmill, the crane's pulleys were worked by means of two large treadmills operated by children – a grim existence by any measure. Installed in 1290 – and only dismantled in 1767 – the crane impressed visitors greatly and was taken as a sign of Bruges's economic success. The crane appears in the background of several medieval paintings, notably behind St John in Memling's *St John Altarpiece* (see page 58).

Jan van Eyckplein

MAP P.72, POCKET MAP C4

Jan van Eyckplein is one of the prettiest squares in Bruges, its cobblestones backdropped by the easy sweep of the Spiegelrei canal. The centrepiece of the square is an earnest **statue** of Van Eyck, erected in 1878, whilst on the north side is the **Tolhuis**, whose fancy

North and east of the Markt

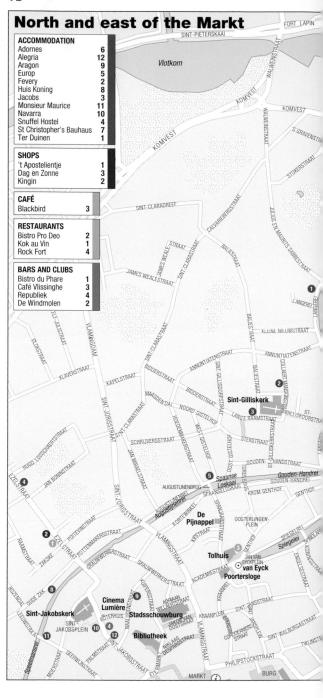

ACCOMMODATION

Adornes	6
Alegria	12
Aragon	9
Europ	5
Fevery	2
Huis Koning	8
Jacobs	3
Monsieur Maurice	11
Navarra	10
Snuffel Hostel	4
St Christopher's Bauhaus	7
Ter Duinen	1

SHOPS

't Apostelientje	1
Dag en Zonne	3
Kingin	2

CAFÉ

Blackbird	3

RESTAURANTS

Bistro Pro Deo	2
Kok au Vin	1
Rock Fort	4

BARS AND CLUBS

Bistro du Phare	1
Café Vlissinghe	3
Republiek	4
De Windmolen	2

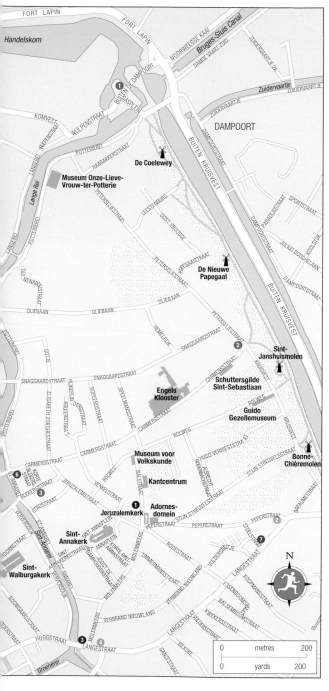

FORT LAPIN

FORT LAPIN

Handelskom

Bruges-Sluis Canal

NOORWEEGSE KAAI

DAMSE VAART-ZUID

ZUIDERVAARTJE

ZUIDERVAARTJE-2A

Zuidervaartje

ZUIDERVAARTJE

KOMVEST

WULPENSTRAAT

BUITEN DE DAMPOORT

DAMPLEIN

ZUIDERVAARTJE

DAMPOORT

DAMPOORTSTRAAT

LANGEREI

POTTERIEREI

HAARAKKERSTRAAT

De Coelewey

BUITEN KRUISVEST

Lange Rei

POTTERIEREI

Museum Onze-Lieve-
Vrouw-ter-Potterie

PETERSELIESTRAAT

LEESTENBURG

OOST-PROOSSE

PARADIJSSTRAAT

SPORTSTRAAT

DAMPOORTSTRAAT

JULIUS DOOGHELAAN

KOOLSTUK

QUI

NENABOSTRAAT

PEREGAANISTRAAT

PETERSELIESTRAAT

De Nieuwe
Papegaal

BUITEN KRUISVEST

DAMPOORTSTRAAT

OLIEBAAN

OLIEBAAN

OLIEBAAN

HEMELRIJK

PETERSELIESTRAAT

POTTERIEREI

DOTJE

NENABOSTRAAT

SNAGGAARDSTRAAT

Sint-
Janshuismolen

POTTERIEREI

SNAGGAARDSTRAAT

RIJKEPIJNDERSTRAAT

ROPEERDSTRAAT

SPEELMANSSTRAAT

SNAGGAARDSTRAAT

CARMERSSTRAAT

Schuttersgilde
Sint-Sebastiaan

ELISABETH ZORGHESTRAAT

KRUISVEST

KRUISSTRAAK

Engels
Klooster

CARMERSSTRAAT

ROLWEG

Guido
Gezellemuseum

POTTERIEREI

CARMERSSTRAAT

CARMERSSTRAAT

ROLWEG

Bonne-
Chièremolen

KRUISVEST

Museum voor
Volkskunde

ROLWEG

HUGO VERRIESTSTRAAT

STIJN STREUVELSSTRAAT

BALSTRAAT

VENKELSTRAAT

Kantcentrum

ALBRECHT
RODENBACHSTRAAT

BAPAUMESTRAAT

CARMERSSTRAAT

JERUZALEMSTRAAT

Adornes-
domein

STIJN STREUVELSSTRAAT

PEPERSTRAAT

BLEKERSSTRAAT

BALGERS
STRAAT

KORTE

Jeruzalemkerk

SINT-ANNAPLEIN

PEPERSTRAAT

PEPERSTRAAT

STROBRUGGE

STIJN STREUVELSSTRAAT

STROSTRAAT

S.ANNAREI

Sint-
Annakerk

KORTE SINT-
ANNASTRAAT

RODESTRAAT

VOLDERSBRIJKE

LANGESTRAAT

STEELSTRAAT

N

VERVERSDIJK

SINT-ANNASTRAAT

SINT-
ANNAPLEIN

MOLENMEERS

TIMMERMANSSTRAAT

KOOPMANSSTRAAT

HOOGSTRAAT

SINT-ANNAREI

OOST DE
DAMHOUDERSTRAAT

VERBRAND NIEUWLAND

ESSEABOOMSTRAAT

Sint-
Walburgakerk

VERVERSDIJK

MOLENMEERS

LANGESTRAAT

ESSEABOOMSTRAAT

BALSEMBOOMSTRAAT

BOOMGAARDSTRAAT

VERBRAND NIEUWLAND

VLADERSTRAAT

KWEKERSSTRAAT

HOOGSTRAAT

MOLENMEERS

LANGESTRAAT

BILKSE

GANZESTRAAT

Groenerei

0		metres		200
0		yards		200

The Spiegelrei canal

Renaissance entrance is decorated with the coat of arms of the dukes of Luxembourg, who long levied tolls here. The Tolhuis dates from the late fifteenth century, but was extensively remodelled in medieval style in the 1870s, as was the **Poortersloge** (Merchants' Lodge), whose slender tower pokes up above the rooftops on the west side of the square. Theoretically, each and every city merchant was entitled to be a member of the Poortersloge, but in fact membership was restricted to the richest and the most powerful. An informal alternative to the Town Hall, it was here that key political and economic decisions were taken and it was also where local bigwigs could drink and gamble discreetly away from prying eyes.

The Spiegelrei canal and around

MAP P.72, POCKET MAP D4

Running east from Jan van Eyckplein, the **Spiegelrei canal** was once the heart of the foreign merchants' quarter, its frenetic quays overlooked by the trade missions of many of the city's trading partners. The medieval buildings framing the canal were demolished long ago, but they have been replaced by an exquisite medley of architectural styles from expansive Classical mansions through to the more modest brick dwellings of lesser merchants, who dug deep into their pockets for the pirouetting crow-step gables that adorn their former homes today. At the far end of Spiegelrei, a left turn brings you onto one of the city's loveliest streets, **Gouden-Handrei**, which, along with adjoining **Spaanse Loskaai**, was once the focus of the Spanish merchants' district. On the far side of the canal stand a string of delightful summer outhouses, privately owned and sometimes surprisingly lavish extensions to the demure houses fronting onto Gouden-Handstraat. The west end of Spaanse Loskaai is marked by the **Augustijnenbrug**, the city's oldest surviving bridge, a sturdy three-arched structure dating from 1391. The bridge was built to help the monks of a nearby (and long-demolished) Augustinian monastery get into the city centre speedily; the benches set into the parapet were cut to allow itinerant tradesmen to display their goods here.

Spanjaardstraat

MAP P.72, POCKET MAP C4
Running south from the
Augustijnenbrug bridge (see
above) is narrow **Spanjaardstraat**,
which was also part of the Spanish
merchants' enclave – hence the
platoon of substantial terrace
houses. It was here, at no.9, in
a house formerly known as **De
Pijnappel** (The Fir Cone), that the
founder of the Jesuits, the Spaniard
Ignatius Loyola (1491–1556),
spent his holidays while he was a
student in Paris in the early 1530s.
He befriended Juan Luis Vives
(see page 47), who lodged down
the street, but unfortunately his
friend's liberality – relatively, at
least, he did after all proclaim that
"an unmarried woman should
rarely appear in public" – failed to
temper Loyola's nascent fanaticism.
Spanjaardstraat leads back to Jan
van Eyckplein (see page 50).

St-Gilliskerk

MAP P.72, POCKET MAP D3–D4
Baliestraat ☎ 050 44 87 43, ⓦ visitbruges.
be. April–Sept Mon–Sat 10am–noon &
2–5pm, Sun 2–5pm; Oct–March daily
2–5pm. Free.
The sturdy brick pile of **St-
Gilliskerk** dates from the late
thirteenth century, though it was
considerably enlarged in the 1460s;
the church has a wide and appealing
three-aisled nave, but its most
distinctive feature is its barrel-
vaulted roof, which was added in
the eighteenth century. Among
the **paintings**, the pick is the
Hemelsdale polyptych by the prolific
Pieter Pourbus – on the wall just
to the right of the main doors. It's
a dainty piece of work with the
donors at either end sandwiching
four scenes from the life of Christ:
the *Adoration of the Shepherds*, the
Arrival of the Magi, the *Flight into
Egypt* and Jesus' *Circumcision*. The
church also possesses six eighteenth-
century paintings illustrating the
efforts of the Trinitarian monks to
ransom Christian prisoners from the
Turks. The paintings are distinctly
second-rate, but the two near the
organ in the top right-hand corner
of the church are interesting in their
sinister representation of the east
– all glowering clouds and gloomy
city walls. The other four paintings,
in the bottom left-hand corner of
the nave, illustrate the 1198 papal
foundation of the Trinitarians, an
order devoted to the ransom of
Christians held by Muslims, and
one which enjoyed support from
St-Gilliskerk.

St-Walburgakerk

MAP P.72, POCKET MAP D5
St-Maartensplein, off Koningstraat ☎ 050
44 87 43, ⓦ visitbruges.be. April–Sept
Mon–Sat 10am–noon & 2–5pm, Sun
2–5pm; Oct–March daily 2–5pm. Free.
Southeast of Jan van Eyckplein, **St-
Walburgakerk** is a fluent Baroque
extravagance built for the Jesuits
in the first half of the seventeenth
century. Framed by slender
pilasters, the sinuous, flowing
facade is matched by the stunning
extravagance of the booming
interior, awash with acres of
creamy-white paint. The grandiose
pulpit, complete with its huffing

A painting by Jan Maes in St-Gilliskerk

and puffing cherubs, was the work of Artus II Quellin (1625–1700), an Antwerp woodcarver and sculptor whose family ran a profitable sideline in Baroque pulpits. The pick of the church's scattering of **paintings** is a triptych by **Pieter Claeissens the Younger** (1535–1623) on the right-hand side of the nave. The central panel depicts a popular legend relating to Philip the Good, a fifteenth-century count of Flanders and the founder of the Order of the Golden Fleece (see page 61). The story goes that as Philip was preparing to fight the French, he encountered the Virgin Mary in a scorched tree; not one to look a gift horse in the mouth, Philip fell to his knees and asked for victory, and his prayers were duly answered.

St-Annakerk

MAP P.72, POCKET MAP E4
St-Annaplein ☎ 050 44 87 43,
ⓦ visitbruges.be. April–Sept Mon–Sat
10am–noon & 2–5pm, Sun 2–5pm; Oct–
March daily 2–5pm. Free.

Founded in the 1490s, **St-Annakerk** came a cropper in the religious wars of the sixteenth century when the Protestants burnt the place to the ground. Rebuilt in the 1620s, the church is a dinky little structure surmounted by the slenderest of brick towers and set within a pleasant little square. Almost untouched since its reconstruction, the interior is a notably homogeneous example of the Baroque, its barrel-vaulted, single-aisle nave almost drowning in ornately carved, dark-stained wooden panelling. Pride of artistic place going to the marble and porphyry rood screen of 1628, but you can't miss the huge painting of the *Last Judgement*, hung above the entrance in 1685 and the finest surviving painting by the Flemish artist **Hendrik Herregouts** (1633–1724). Born near Antwerp, Herregouts was an artistic star of the counter-Reformation, painting religious scenes in a score of churches across Dutch-speaking Belgium, but it was in Bruges that

St-Annakerk

Bruges's medieval gates – and a windmill or two

Medieval Bruges had seven **gates** interrupting the wall and moat that encircled the city and although the wall has almost entirely disappeared – unlike the moat – four of the gates have survived in good condition. All four date from the late-fourteenth and early-fifteenth centuries, though each has been heavily restored. Of the four, the two prettiest are the **Smedenpoort**, on the west side of the city centre at the end of Smedenstraat, and the **Ezelpoort** (Donkey Gate), to the northwest of the centre, both of which exhibit twin, heavily fortified towers, rising above the moat. The **Gentpoort** (☎ 050 44 87 11, ⊚ visitbruges.be; Tues–Sun 9.30am–12.30pm & 1.30–5pm; €4), on the southeast edge of the centre on Gentpoortstraat, has twin circular brick towers on one side and a church-like facade on the other. The niche statue on the facade is of St Adrian, an early fourth-century figure and member of the Praetorian guard, who was so impressed by the Christians he was torturing that he was converted – and subsequently martyred. The interior of the Gentpoort holds a mildly diverting museum exploring how the city ramparts and gates developed and evolved. There is also a collection of incidental weaponry and you can access the roof for the view. Almost identical to the Gentpoort is the fourth and final surviving gate, the **Kruispoort**, at the far end of Langestraat. Belgium's assorted invaders have usually chosen to enter Bruges via this gate – including the Habsburg Charles V, Napoleon and the German army (twice). Perched on top of the earthen bank near the Kruispoort are a quartet of **windmills** – two clearly visible and another two beyond eyeshot, about 300m and 500m to the north. You'd have to be something of a windmill fanatic to want to visit them all, but the nearest two are mildly diverting – and the closest, **St-Janshuismolen**, is in working order, and the only one that is open (☎ 050 44 87 43, ⊚ visitbruges.be; April–Sept Tues–Sun 9.30am–12.30pm & 1.30–5pm; €3).

he was most popular, living in the city from 1680 to 1690.

Adornesdomein: the Jeruzalemkerk

MAP P.72, POCKET MAP E4
Peperstraat 3 ☎ 050 33 88 83, ⊚ adornes.org. Mon–Sat 10am–5pm. €7.

Beyond the Spiegelrei canal is an old working-class district, whose simple brick cottages surround the **Adornesdomein**, a substantial complex of buildings belonging to the wealthy Adornes family, who migrated here from Genoa in the thirteenth century and then proceeded to make a fortune

from alum, a special sort of dye fastener made from a hydrated double sulphate. A visit to the *domein* begins towards the rear of the complex, where a set of humble brick almshouses hold a small **museum**, which gives the historical low-down on the family. The most interesting figure was **Anselm Adornes** (1424–1483), whose rollercoaster career included high-power diplomatic missions to Scotland and being punished for corruption – he was fined and paraded through Bruges dressed only in his underwear. Anselm and one of his sons also made the

perilous pilgrimage to the Holy
Land, where they were much
impressed by the Church of the
Holy Sepulchre in Jerusalem.
On their return, they decided to
commission an approximate copy
of the church they had visited
and the result is the idiosyncratic
Jeruzalemkerk (Jerusalem Church)
that now dominates the *domein*.
The church's interior is on two
levels: the lower one features a large
and ghoulish altarpiece, decorated
with skulls and ladders, in front
of which is the black marble
mausoleum of Anselm Adornes
and his wife Margaretha – though
the only part of Anselm held here
is his heart: Anselm was murdered
in Scotland, which is where he was
buried, but his heart was sent back
to Bruges. There's more grisliness
at the back of the church, where
the small vaulted chapel holds a
replica of Christ's tomb – you can
glimpse the imitation body down
the tunnel behind the iron grating.
To either side of the main altar,
steps ascend to the choir, which is
situated right below the eccentric,
onion-domed lantern tower.

The Jeruzalemkerk

Kantcentrum

MAP P.72, POCKET MAP E4
Balstraat 16 ☎ 050 33 00 72,
Ⓦ kantcentrum.eu. Mon–Sat 9.30am–5pm.
Demonstrations Mon–Sat 2–5pm. €5.20,
including demonstrations.

The ground floor of the
Kantcentrum (Lace Centre), just
metres from the Adornesdomein,
traces the history of the lace
industry here in Bruges and displays
a substantial sample of antique,
handmade lace. The earliest major
piece is an exquisite, seventeenth-
century Lenten veil with scenes
from the life of Ignatius of Loyola,
the founder of the Jesuits, and
there are also seventeenth- and
eighteenth-century collars, ruffs and
fans of great delicacy.

Indeed, Belgian lace – or
Flanders lace as it was formerly
known – was renowned for the
fineness of its thread and beautiful
motifs and it was once worn in
all the courts of Europe. It was in
the nineteenth century, however,
that the Bruges lace industry
took a surprising turn. Right
across Flanders, lace had always
played second commercial fiddle
to linen manufacture, but in the
1830s British clothiers undercut
and overwhelmed their Flemish
competitors and the results were
catastrophic, with thousands of
Flemish spinners and weavers
left destitute; poor harvests and
epidemics of cholera and typhus
made things even worse. In these
dire circumstances, the Catholic
church – or rather its parish priests
– and Belgium's liberal bourgeoisie
swallowed their mutual hatred
to step into the breach, training
hundreds of Flemish women in
the art of **lace-making** in scores
of convents and specialist schools.
It might have seemed a foolish
initiative, given that **machine-
made lace** was very much on
the rise, but there was a market
for certain sorts of handmade
lace – Flemish Valenciennes and
Chantilly, for example – and

Lace-making at Kantcentrum

the expansion of the Bruges lace industry did mitigate the worst effects of the economic collapse. There was an ideological point, too: for the clergy, the home-working female lace maker, who was usually trained by nuns, was the epitome of domestic virtue, whereas, for Belgium's liberals and socialists, the badly paid and poorly educated Flemish lace maker was a symbol of exploitation – and the difference of opinion fuelled bitter debate.

At the start of the twentieth century, there were 47,000 lace-makers in Belgium, of whom over 30,000 were in Bruges, but the industry collapsed after World War I when lace, a symbol of an old and discredited order, suddenly had no place in the wardrobe of most women. Nowadays, lace-making is a local tradition-cum-hobby and there are **demonstrations** of handmade lace-making upstairs at the Kantcentrum. You can buy pieces here too – or stroll along the street to the excellent *'t Apostelientje* (see page 86).

Museum voor Volkskunde

MAP P.72, POCKET MAP E4
Balstraat 43 ☏ 050 44 87 43, ⓦ visit bruges.be. Tues–Sun 9.30am–5pm. €6.

The unassuming **Museum voor Volkskunde** (Folklore Museum) occupies a long line of low-ceilinged almshouses set beside a trim courtyard. The interior is parcelled up into small period rooms, with the emphasis on the nineteenth and early twentieth centuries, but the labelling is patchy so it's best to pick up an English guidebook at reception. There's also a small tavern, *De Zwarte Kat* (The Black Cat), done out in traditional style and serving ales and average snacks. Room 1 features an old classroom circa 1920, but the first high spot is Room 5, which focuses on popular religion and displays an interesting collection of pilgrimage banners as well as the wax, silver and iron ex votos that still hang in many Flemish churches. With the ex voto, the believer makes a promise to God – say, to behave better – and then asks for a blessing, like the curing of a bad leg. Sometimes the ex voto is hung up once the promise is made, but mostly it's done afterwards, in gratitude for the cure or blessing. Further on in the museum, Room 8 holds a display on pipes and tobacco. There are all sorts of antique

Exhibition at the Museum voor Volkskunde

smokers' paraphernalia – tobacco cutters, lighters, tinder boxes and so forth – but it's the pipes that catch the eye, especially the long, thin ones made of clay. Clay pipes were notoriously brittle, so smokers invested in pipe cases, of which several are displayed. Room 12 is an old confectioner's shop, where there are occasional demonstrations of traditional sweet-making in summertime, and the next room holds a mildly diverting assortment of biscuit and chocolate moulds as well as cake decorations (*patacons*). Made of clay, these *patacons* were painted by hand in true folksy style, with the three most popular motifs being animals, military scenes and Bible stories.

The Guido Gezellemuseum

Map p.72, POCKET MAP F3.
Rolweg 64 ☏ 050 44 87 43, ⓦ visitbruges.be.
Tues–Sun 9.30am–12.30pm & 1.30–5pm. €4.
The **Guido Gezellemuseum** commemorates the poet-priest Guido Gezelle (1830–99), a leading figure in nineteenth-century Bruges. Gezelle was born in this large brick cottage, which now contains a few personal knick-knacks such as Gezelle's old chair and pipes, plus his death mask, though it's mostly devoted to a biographical account of his life. The labelling is, however, only in Dutch and you really need to be a Gezelle enthusiast to get much out of it. Neither is Gezelle to everyone's taste. His poetry is pretty average and the fact that he translated Longfellow's *Song of Hiawatha* into Dutch is the sort of detail that bores rather than inspires.

More importantly, Gezelle played a key role in the preservation of many of the city's medieval buildings, believing that the survival of the medieval city symbolized the continuity of the Catholic faith, a mindset similar to that of the city's Flemish nationalists, who resisted change and championed medieval – or at least neo-Gothic – architecture to maintain Flemish "purity". Gezelle resisted cultural change, too: secular theatre appalled him, prompting him to write: "We are smothered by displays of adultery and incest… and the foundations of the family and of marriage are [being] undermined".

Schuttersgilde St-Sebastiaan

MAP P.72, POCKET MAP E3
Carmersstraat 174 ☏ 050 33 16 26,
ⓦ sebastiaansgilde.be. May–Sept Tues–
Thurs 10am–noon, Sat 2–5pm; Oct–April
Tues–Thurs & Sat 2–5pm. €3.

The guild house of the
Schuttersgilde St-Sebastiaan –
The Marksmen's (or Archers') Guild
of St Sebastian – is a large brick pile
with a distinctive tower dating from
the middle of the sixteenth century.
The city's archers had ceased to be
of any military importance by the
time of its construction, but the
guild had, by then, redefined itself
as an exclusive social club where
the bigwigs of the day could spend
their time hobnobbing. Nowadays,
it's still in use as a social-cum-sports
club where the archers opting either
to shoot at the familiar circular
targets or to plonk a replica bird
on top of a pole and shoot at
it from below – the traditional
favourite. All in all, the house is
hardly riveting, but it does possess
an attractive old dining hall, where
a bust of Charles II surmounts the
fireplace, recalling the days when
the exiled king was a guild member

(see page 83). Visitors can also
drop by the shooting gallery, whose
medievalist stained-glass windows
date from the 1950s, and peek at
the modern clubhouse.

Engels Klooster

MAP P.72, POCKET MAP E3
Carmersstraat 85 ☏ 050 33 24 24, ⓦ the-
english-convent.be. Mon–Thurs & Sat
2–3.30pm & 4.30–5.30pm. Free.

During his stay in Bruges, the
exiled king Charles II (see page
83) worshipped more or less
regularly here at the **Engels
Klooster** (English Convent) on
Carmersstraat. Founded in 1629,
the convent was long a haven for
English Catholic exiles, though
this didn't deter the very Protestant
Queen Victoria from popping
in during her visit to Belgium in
1843. Nowadays, the convent's
nuns provide an enthusiastic
fifteen-minute guided tour of the
lavishly decorated Baroque church,
whose finest features are the
handsome cupola and the altar, an
extraordinarily flashy affair made
of 23 different types of marble – a
gift of the Nithsdales, English
aristocrats whose loyalty to the

Schuttersgilde St-Sebastiaan

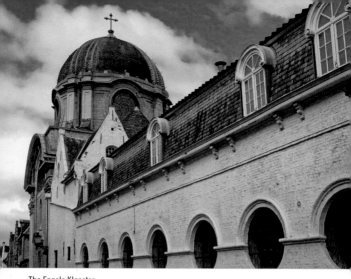

The Engels Klooster

Catholic faith got them into no end of trouble.

Museum Onze-Lieve-Vrouw-ter-Potterie

MAP P.72, POCKET MAP D2
Potterierei 79 ☎ 050 44 87 43,
ⓦ visitbruges.be. Tues–Sun 9.30am–
12.30pm & 1.30–5pm. €6.
The **Museum Onze-Lieve-Vrouw-ter-Potterie** (Museum of Our Lady of the Pottery) was founded as a hospital in the thirteenth century on the site of an earlier pottery – hence the name. The hospital (though "hospital" is a tad misleading, as the buildings were originally used as much to accommodate visitors as tend the sick) was remodelled on several occasions and the three brick gables that front the building today span three centuries. The middle gable is the oldest, dating from 1359 and built as part of the first hospital chapel. The left-hand gable belonged to the main medieval hospital ward and the one on the right marks a second chapel, added in the 1620s. Inside, a visit begins in the former **sick room**, where a selection of medieval religious paintings includes several anonymous triptychs and a small but arresting panel-painting of *St Michael triumphing over the Devil*, by the Master of the St Ursula Legend.

Moving on, the museum's **chapel** is an L-shaped affair distinguished by a sumptuous marble rood screen, whose two side-altars recall the museum's location beside what was once one of the city's busiest quays. The altar on the left is dedicated to St Anthony, the patron saint of ships' joiners, the one on the right to St Brendan, the patron saint of seamen. There's also a finely expressed thirteenth-century stone statue of the Virgin on the main altar, but pride of place goes to the set of old **tapestries** that are hung in the chapel from Easter to October. These comprise a superbly naturalistic, brightly coloured cartoon strip depicting eighteen miracles attributed to Our Lady of the Pottery, almost all to do with being saved from the sea or a sudden change of fortune in fishing or trade. Each carries an inscription, but you'll need to be good at Dutch to decipher them.

Charles II in Bruges

Charles II of England, who spent three years in exile in Bruges from 1656 to 1659, was an enthusiastic member of the archers' guild and, after the Restoration, he sent them a whopping 3600 florins as a thank you for their hospitality. Charles's enforced exile had begun in 1651 after his attempt to seize the English crown – following the Civil War and the execution of his father in 1649 – had ended in defeat by the Parliamentarians at the Battle of Worcester. Initially, Charles high-tailed it to France, but Cromwell persuaded the French to expel him and the exiled king ended up seeking sanctuary in Spanish territory. He was allowed to settle in **Bruges**, then part of the Spanish Netherlands, though the Habsburgs were stingy when it came to granting Charles and his retinue an allowance. The royalists were, says a courtier's letter of 1657, "never in greater want... for Englishmen cannot live on bread alone". In addition, Cromwell's spies kept an eagle eye on Charles's activities, filing lurid reports about his conduct. A certain Mr Butler informed Cromwell that "I think I may truly say that greater abominations were never practised among people than at Charles Stuart's court. Fornication, drunkenness and adultery are considered no sins amongst them." It must have made Cromwell's hair stand on end. Cromwell died of malaria in 1658 and Charles was informed of this whilst he was playing tennis in Bruges. The message was to the point – "The devil is dead" – and Charles was on the English throne two years later. Neither did Charles's hatred of Cromwell end with the Protector's death: Charles had Cromwell disinterred and posthumously executed.

Museum Onze-Lieve-Vrouw-ter-Potterie

Belgian beer: top brews

These tasting notes should help you through the (very pleasurable) maze that is **Belgian beer** – this is, after all, a country where many bars have **beer menus**.

Brugse Zot (Blond 6, Brugse Zot Dubbel 7.5)
Brouwerij De Halve Mann, a small brewery located in the centre of Bruges (see page 63), produces refreshing ales with a dry, crisp aftertaste. Their Blond is a light and tangy pale ale, whereas the Bruin – Brugse Zot Dubbel – is a classic brown ale with a full body.

Bush Beer (7.5 and 12) A Walloon speciality. At 12, it's claimed that the original version is the strongest beer in Belgium. It's actually more like a barley wine, with a lovely golden colour and an earthy aroma. The 7.5 Bush is a tasty pale ale with a hint of coriander.

Chimay (red top 7, blue top 9) Made by Trappist monks in southern Belgium, Chimay beers are regarded as among the best in the world. Of their several brews, these two are the most readily available, fruity and strong, deep in body, and somewhat spicy with a hint of nutmeg and thyme.

La Chouffe (8) Produced in the Ardennes, this distinctive beer is instantly recognizable by the red-hooded gnome *chouffe* that adorns its label. It's a refreshing pale ale with a peachy aftertaste.

Gouden Carolus (8) Named after – and allegedly the favourite tipple of – the Habsburg emperor Charles V, Gouden Carolus is a full-bodied dark brown ale with a sour and slightly fruity aftertaste. Brewed in Mechelen.

Hoegaarden (5) The role model for all Belgian wheat beers, Hoegaarden, from near Leuven, is light and extremely refreshing, despite its cloudy appearance. The ideal drink for a hot summer's day, it's brewed from equal parts of wheat and malted barley.

Kriek (Cantillon Kriek Lambic 5, Belle Vue Kriek 5.2, Mort Subite Kriek 4.3) A type of beer made from a base lambic beer to which are added cherries or cherry juice and perhaps even sugar. Other fruit beers are available, such as Framboise. The better versions (including the three mentioned above) are not too sweet and taste wonderful.

Orval (6.2) One of the world's most distinctive malt beers, Orval is made in the Ardennes at the Abbaye d'Orval. Refreshingly bitter, the beer is a lovely amber colour and makes a great aperitif.

Rochefort (Rochefort 6 7.5, Rochefort 8 9.2, Rochefort 10 11.3) Produced at a Trappist monastery in the Ardennes, Rochefort beers are typically dark and sweet and come in three main versions: Rochefort 6, Rochefort 8 and the extremely popular Rochefort 10, which has a deep reddish-brown colour and a delicious fruity palate.

Rodenbach (Rodenbach 5 and Rodenbach Grand Cru 6.5) The Rodenbach brewery produces a reddish-brown ale in several forms, with the best brews aged in oak containers. Their widely available Rodenbach is a tangy brown ale with a hint of sourness. The much fuller – and sourer – Rodenbach Grand Cru is more difficult to get hold of, but delicious.

Westmalle (Westmalle Dubbel 7, Tripel 9) The Trappist monks of Westmalle, just north of Antwerp, claim their beers not only cure loss of appetite and insomnia, but reduce stress. Whatever the truth, the prescription certainly tastes good. Their most famous beer, Westmalle Tripel, is creamy and aromatic, while the Westmalle Dubbel is dark and supremely malty.

Lambic beers

One of the world's oldest styles of beer manufacture, Brussels' **lambic** beers are tart brews made with at least thirty percent raw wheat with malted barley. **Wild yeast** is used in their production, a process of spontaneous fermentation in which the yeasts – specific to the air of Brussels – gravitate down into open wooden casks over a period of two to three years. Draught lambic is rare, but the bottled varieties are more commonplace. **Cantillon Lambic** is perhaps the most authentic, an excellent drink with a lemony zip. It's the best you'll find (5).**Gueuze** is a blend of old and new lambics in a bottle, a little sweeter and fuller bodied than straight lambic, with an almost cider-like aftertaste. Other good brews include Belle Vue Gueuze (5.2), Timmermans Gueuze (5.5) and Lindemans Gueuze (5.2)

Bistro Pro Deo

Shops

't Apostelientje

MAP P.72, POCKET MAP E4
Balstraat 11 ☎ 050 33 78 60,
Ⓦ apostelientje.be. Tues 1.15–5pm, Wed–Sat 9.30am–12.15pm & 1.15–5pm, Sun 9.30am–12.15pm.

This small and infinitely cosy shop sells a charming variety of handmade lace pieces of both modern and traditional design. It's easily the best lace shop in Bruges with extremely helpful and well-informed staff. The smallest pieces cost €20.

Dag en Zonne

MAP P.72, POCKET MAP E5
Langestraat 3 ☎ 050 33 02 93. Daily except Sun & Wed 2–6pm.

Tiny and cramped Aladdin's cave of a place, jam-packed with all sorts of inexpensive trinkets and baubles. There are clocks and barometers, vintage prints, antique tiles, shot glasses, pieces of stained glass, pottery, a good selection of second-hand jewellery, plus all sorts of once-treasured bygones.

Kingin

MAP P.72, POCKET MAP B4
Ezelstraat 27 ☎ 050 34 19 09, Ⓦ kingin.be.
Tues–Fri 2–6.30pm & Sat 9.30am–12.30pm & 1.30–6.30pm.

Hand-made, top-quality jewellery is on sale here at this chic little shop on the north side of the city centre. Gold, silver and precious stones are to the fore – and the designs range from the more straightforward to the ambitious and positively daring. Predictably, it's expensive.

Café

Blackbird

MAP P.72, POCKET MAP C4
Jan van Eyckplein 7 ☎ 0471 67 98 31, Ⓦ blackbird-bruges.com. Wed–Sat 9am–5pm, Sun 9.30am–1pm.

This bright and welcoming café, with its inventive modern décor, throws a wide gastronomic net: breakfasts feature all manner of healthy options (€12), and there are sandwiches (€14), plus superb lunch-time salads, heaped high and very fresh (€16). They also do creative side-lines in Spanish-style tapas and even cocktails.

Restaurants

Bistro Pro Deo

MAP P.72, POCKET MAP F4
Langestraat 161 ☎ 050 33 73 55, Ⓦ bistroprodeo.be. Tues–Fri noon–2pm & 6–9.30pm, Sat 6–10pm.

This pocket-sized, bistro-style restaurant is a local favourite, its enterprising menu emphasizing traditional Flemish cuisine: try, for example, the filling *stoofvlees* (Flemish beef stew) for just €20. The decor is folksy and there's a jazz meets soul soundtrack.

Kok au Vin

MAP P.72, POCKET MAP B4
Ezelstraat 21 ☎ 050 33 95 21, Ⓦ kok-au-vin.be. Tues–Sat noon–2pm & 6.30–9.30pm.

Smart restaurant occupying tastefully modernized old premises. A well-considered and ambitious menu covers all the Franco-Belgian bases and then some, with mains averaging around €25, though lunch is half that. Try the signature dish – coq au vin. Reservations highly recommended.

Rock Fort

MAP P.72, POCKET MAP E5
Langestraat 15 ☏ 050 33 41 13,
ⓦ rock-fort.be. Mon–Fri except Wed noon–2.30pm & 6.30–10.30pm.
Highly regarded restaurant in chic and cool premises just off the normal tourist beat. The creative, international menu of nouvelle cuisine is particularly strong on seafood and shellfish, but there are many other gastronomic delights – try the duck breast and liver paté apple starter. Main courses average around €28.

Bars and clubs

Bistro du Phare

MAP P.72, POCKET MAP E1
Sasplein 2 ☏ 050 34 35 90, ⓦ duphare.be.
Daily except Tues 11am–11.30pm.
Off the beaten track, this busy, bustling place offers filling food, a good range of beers and a canal setting. There's also a pleasant summer terrace and evening jazz and blues concerts every month or so, come early to get a seat.

Café Vlissinghe

MAP P.72, POCKET MAP D4
Blekersstraat 2 ☏ 050 34 37 37,
ⓦ cafevlissinghe.be. Wed–Sat 11am–10pm,
Sun 11am–7pm.
With its wood panelling, antique paintings and long wooden tables, this is one of the oldest and most distinctive bars in Bruges, thought to date from 1515. The atmosphere is relaxed and easy-going, with the emphasis on quiet conversation – there are certainly no jukeboxes here – and the bar snacks are

traditional Flemish. There's a pleasant garden terrace, too.

Republiek

MAP P.72, POCKET MAP C5
St-Jakobsstraat 36 ☏ 050 73 47 64,
ⓦ republiekbrugge.be Daily noon–1/2am.
One of the most popular café-bars in town, this large and darkly lit café-bar attracts an arty, mostly youthful clientele. Very reasonably priced snacks and light meals, including vegetarian and pasta dishes, plus the occasional gig. There's a terrace at the back for summertime drinking.

De Windmolen

MAP P.72, POCKET MAP F3
Carmersstraat 135 ☏ 050 33 97 39.
Mon–Thurs 10am–10pm, Fri & Sun 10am–3pm.
This amiable, neighbourhood café-bar is a pick for its setting – away from the crowds and next to the grassy bank that marks the course of the old city wall. It dishes up a pretty average line in inexpensive snacks but there's a competent beer menu and a pleasant outside terrace.

De Windmolen

Damme

Now a popular day-trippers' destination, the quaint village of Damme, 7km northeast of Bruges, was in medieval times the city's main seaport, but those heady days are long gone. Today, Damme has just one main street, Kerkstraat, a few minutes' walk from end to end, and to either side are what remains of the medieval town, principally the Stadhuis (Town Hall) and the Onze Lieve Vrouwekerk (Church of Our Lady). A pretty, poplar-lined canal connects Bruges and Damme, starting at Dampoort on the northeast edge of central Bruges and trimming the edge of Damme before proceeding onto Sluis, a tiny village over the border in the Netherlands. This Bruges-Sluis canal slices its way across a delightful parcel of countryside, a rural backwater of green fields and whitewashed farmhouses, all shadowed by long lines of slender poplar trees, quivering and rustling in the prevailing westerly winds. It's perfect cycling country and there are lots of possible routes to explore (see page 92).

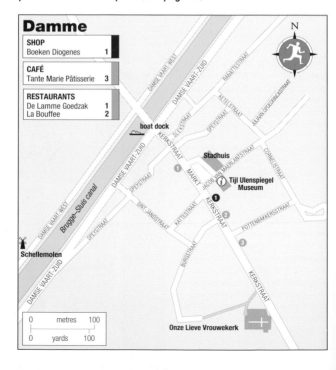

Arrival and information

There are several ways of reaching **Damme from Bruges**, perhaps the most rewarding being the seven-kilometre cycle ride out along the **Brugge–Sluis canal**, which begins at Dampoort, about 2.5km northeast of the Markt. Cycle rental is available in Bruges (see page 140). If you want to explore the area in depth, you should buy a detailed cycling map; the **Fietsnetwerk Brugse Ommeland** (1:50,000), available from any major bookshop in Bruges, is the best choice.

You can also get from Bruges to Damme on a vintage **canal boat**, the *Lamme Goedzak*, with excursions starting about 500m east of the Dampoort on the Noorweegse Kaai (May–Sept Tues–Sun 4 daily each way, plus some sailings at Easter; 45min; one-way €8.50, return €11.50; tickets are purchased on board; ⓦbootdamme-brugge.be). Connecting **bus #4** from Bruges's Markt and the main bus/train station runs to the Noorweegse Kaai to meet most departures, but check at the De Lijn information kiosk, outside the bus/train station, before you set out.

Finally, you can reach Damme on **city bus #43** from the bus station, but it is a very poor service that fluctuates with the school terms and holidays – and even if you can get out there, you can't always get back. Again, check at the De Lijn information kiosk. Damme has its own **tourist office**, across the street from the Stadhuis at Jacob van Maerlantstraat 3 (April–Sept Mon–Fri & Sun 10am–noon & 1–6pm, Sat 10am–noon & 2–6pm; Oct–March Mon–Fri 10am–noon & 1–5pm, Sat & Sun 2–5pm. ☏050 28 86 10, ⓦvisitdamme.be).

Stadhuis, Damme

The Stadhuis

MAP P.88

Markt 1, off Kerkstraat. No public access.

Funded by a special tax on barrels of herrings, the fifteenth-century **Stadhuis** is easily the best-looking building in Damme, its elegant, symmetrical facade balanced by the graceful lines of its exterior stairway. In one of the niches you'll spy Charles the Bold, the last Duke of Burgundy, offering a wedding ring to Margaret of York, who stands in the next niche along – appropriately enough, as the couple got spliced here in 1468, a prestige event that attracted aristocratic bigwigs from all over western Europe. It was Charles's third marriage – his previous wives had died young – and it was one that greatly irritated the French king: the last thing Louis XI wanted was the cementing of the alliance between England and

The Battle of Sluys

In the summer of 1340, a **French fleet** assembled in the estuary of the **River Zwin**, near Damme, to prepare for an invasion of England at the start of the Anglo-French **Hundred Years' War**. To combat the threat, however, the English king, Edward III, sailed across the Channel and attacked at dawn. Although they were outnumbered three to one, Edward's fleet won an extraordinary victory, his bowmen causing chaos by showering the French ships with arrows from what was, for them, a safe distance. A foretaste of the Battle of Crécy, there was so little left of the French force that no one dared tell King Philip VI of France, until finally the court jester took matters into his own hands: "Oh! The English cowards! They had not the courage to jump into the sea as our noble Frenchmen did." Philip's reply is not recorded.

his powerful vassal, the Duke of Burgundy. Indeed, Louis sent a fleet to waylay Margaret on her way to Damme, but it failed to locate her. Margaret arrived at a time when Damme boasted a population of ten thousand and played a key strategic role guarding the banks of the River Zwin, which gave Bruges direct access to the sea. The subsequent silting up of the river – and the decline of Damme – have been the subject of much historical debate: some have argued that the silting of the river led to Bruges's decline,

Tijl Ulenspiegel Museum

others that it was the inability of the city to pay for the continued dredging of the river that reflected the downturn.

Tijl Ulenspiegel Museum

MAP P.88

Jacob van Maerlantstraat 3 ☎ 050 28 86 10, ⓦ visitdamme.be. April–Sept Mon–Fri & Sun 10am–noon & 1–6pm, Sat 10am–noon & 2–6pm; Oct–March Mon–Fri 10am–noon & 1–5pm, Sat & Sun 2–5pm. €2.50.

The **Tijl Ulenspiegel Museum**, in the same building as tourist information (see page 145), is devoted to the eponymous folkloric figure, who started out as an obnoxious fool-cum-prankster in Germany in the early fourteenth century. There has been much speculation as to the meaning of his name, but it's usually translated from the original High German as "owl mirror" – itself a somewhat confused version of "arse wiper", as in Ulenspiegel's addiction to all things scatological. Whatever the truth, Ulenspiegel stories spread into Flanders and as they did so he became more of a scoundrel than a joker, until a Belgian author, **Charles de Coster** (1827–79), subverted the legend in his 1867 novel The Legend of the Glorious Adventures of Tyl Ulenspiegel in the Land of Flanders & Elsewhere. Coster turned Ulenspiegel into a seventeenth-century Protestant hero, the embodiment of the Belgian hankering for religious and political freedom. He made Damme his home and added Nele, Ulenspiegel's fiancée, and Lamme Goedzak, a loyal, lazy and good-natured friend, as well as a mother, Soetkin, and a father, Claes. Ulenspiegel becomes the sworn enemy of King Philip II of Spain after the Spanish take Claes prisoner and burn him at the stake.

Onze Lieve Vrouwekerk

MAP P.88

Kerkstraat. April–Sept daily 2–5pm. Free.
☎ **050 28 86 10,** ⓦ **visitdamme.be.**
A sturdy brick structure in classic Gothic style, the **Onze Lieve Vrouwekerk** (Church of Our Lady) is attached to a ruined segment of the original nave (open access) that speaks volumes about Damme's decline: the church was built in the thirteenth century, but when the population shrank it was just too big

Onze Lieve Vrouwekerk

and so the inhabitants abandoned part of the nave and the remnants are now stuck between the present church and its clumpy tower.

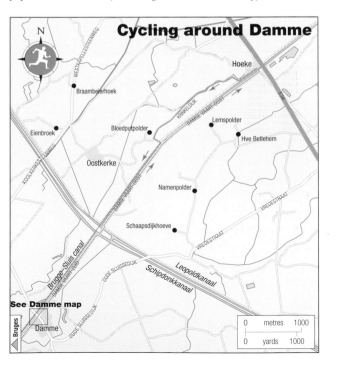

View from the top of Onze-Lieve-Vrouwekerk

Climb the tower for panoramic views over the surrounding polders. Beside the tower, the large and enigmatic, three-headed modern statue, the *Blik van Licht* (Look of Light), is the work of the Belgian painter and sculptor **Charles Delporte** (1928–2012), who had strong connections with Damme. A prolific artist, Delporte had his work displayed all over the world – and nigh-on 300 are exhibited in a variety of locations.

Just beyond the church, on the right-hand side of Kerkstraat, a **footpath** branches off along a narrow canal to loop round the west side of Damme, an enjoyable ten-minute stroll through the poplars which brings you out just west of the village beside the Brugge–Damme-Sluis canal.

Cycling around Damme

Beginning in Bruges at the Dampoort, about 2.5km northeast of the Markt, the country lanes on either side of the **Brugge-Sluis canal** cut a handsome, poplar-lined route across the Flemish countryside. After about 7km, these parallel lanes slip past the northern end of **DAMME**'s main street, Kerkstraat. Thereafter, one especially rewarding cycle route is a 15km-long round-trip that begins by pressing on from Damme along the same, Brugge–Sluis canal. The route then crosses over the wide and murky-green **Leopoldkanaal** before continuing to the tiny and inordinately pretty hamlet of **HOEKE**. Here, just over the bridge, turn hard left for the narrow causeway – the **Krinkeldijk** – which meanders back in the direction of Damme, running just to the north of the Brugge–Sluis canal. Just over 3km long, this causeway drifts across a beguiling landscape of bright whitewashed farmhouses and deep-green grassy fields before reaching an intersection where you turn left to regain the main waterway.

Shop

Boeken Diogenes

MAP P.88

Kerkstraat 22A ☎ 0475 70 16 11, 🌐 visitdamme.be. Late June to late September Tues–Sun 11am–6pm; late Sept to late June Wed–Sun 11am–5pm.

Damme has a handful of tourist-orientated shops, including three art galleries, and, to justify its claim to be a "book town", it possesses half a dozen or so bookshops dotted along the main street and its immediate surroundings. There is also a book market every second Sunday of the month on the main square, Damme Plaats, in the summer and inside the Stadhuis during winter. Amongst the bookshops, *Diogenes* is one of the more diverting, a pocket-sized antiquarian bookshop focusing on literature and art, with many English titles.

Café

Tante Marie Pâtisserie

MAP P.88

Kerkstraat 38 ☎ 050 35 45 03, 🌐 tantemarie.be. Daily 10am–6pm, kitchen from 11.30am.

This pleasant and modern, café-bistro and pâtisserie does an especially delicious line in breakfasts and lunches. The latter features salads and pastas, not to mention one of their specialities, shrimp croquettes. There's also a tasty range of vegetarian options plus a selection of superb pastries – the lemon curd tarts go down a storm. For a full lunch, reckon on around €23.

Restaurants

De Lamme Goedzak

MAP P.88

Kerkstraat 13 ☎ 050 69 22 66, 🌐 delamme goedzak.be. Daily except Tues & Wed

10am–2.30pm & 5.30–9pm.

In attractively refurbished old premises, this is perhaps the best restaurant in Damme – and certainly one of the most popular. The menu covers most of the traditional Flemish dishes – try, for example, the roasted slices of lamb with vegetables. Main courses run the gamut of €25 to €35. Also sells its own house ales and has a garden terrace at the back and a pavement terrace at the front.

La Bouffee

MAP P.88

Kerkstraat 26 ☎ 050 68 05 88, 🌐 labouffee. be. Daily except Tues & Wed noon–2pm & 6.30–9pm.

Intimate and chic, family-owned restaurant offering the most creative of nouvelle cuisine menus. They serve meat and game dishes – the pheasant is delicious – but they specialise in seafood, featuring the likes of salmon with noodles, samphire and peppers. Three courses for €42, four courses €56; also à la carte.

Book market on Damme Plaats

Central Ghent

Ghent may be less immediately picturesque than Bruges, its great and ancient rival, but it still musters a string of superb Gothic buildings and a bevy of delightful, intimate streetscapes, where antique brick houses are woven around a lattice of narrow canals. The city's star turn is undoubtedly St-Baafskathedraal, home to Jan van Eyck's remarkable Adoration of the Mystic Lamb, but it's ably supported by a clutch of other attractions including exquisite medieval guildhouses, enjoyable museums and a brigade of lively bars and first-class restaurants. But perhaps most importantly, Ghent remains a quintessentially Flemish city with a tourist industry – rather than the other way round – and, if you find the tweeness of Bruges overpowering, this is the place to decamp, just twenty minutes away by train.

St-Baafskathedraal

MAP P.96, POCKET MAP D13
St-Baafsplein ☎ 09 269 20 45,
Ⓦ sintbaafskathedraal.be. Cathedral
April–Oct Mon–Sat 8.30am–6pm & Sun
1–6pm; Nov–March Mon–Sat 8.30am–5pm
& Sun 1–5pm; Free. Mystic Lamb April–Oct
Mon–Sat 9.30am–5pm, Sun 1–5pm; Nov–

March Mon–Sat 10.30am–4pm, Sun 1–4pm;
€4. Note that there are plans to move
the Mystic Lamb to another part of the
cathedral in the next year or two.

The best place to start an exploration of the city is the mainly Gothic **St-Baafskathedraal** (St Bavo's Cathedral), squeezed into

The vaulted roof at St-Baafskathedraal

the eastern corner of St-Baafsplein and named after a local seventh-century landowner turned Christian missionary. The third church on this site, and 250 years in the making, the cathedral is a tad lop-sided, but there's no denying the imposing beauty of the **west tower**, with its long, elegant windows and perky corner turrets. Some 82m high, the tower was the last major part of the church to be completed, topped off in 1554 – just before the outbreak of the religious wars that were to wrack the country for the next hundred years.

Inside the cathedral, *The Adoration of the Mystic Lamb* (see page 110) is – at least for the present – displayed in the side-chapel at the start of the mighty fifteenth-century **nave**, whose tall, slender columns give the whole interior a cheerful sense of lightness, though the Baroque marble screen spoils the effect by darkening the choir. In the nave, the principal item of interest is the rococo **pulpit**, a whopping oak and marble affair, where the main timber represents the Tree of Life with an allegorical representation of Time and Truth at its base. Nearby, the **north transept** holds a characteristically energetic painting by **Rubens** (1577–1640) entitled *St Baaf entering the Abbey of Ghent*. Dating to 1624, when **Rubens** was at the height of his fame and a favourite of the Spanish Habsburgs, the painting includes a self-portrait – he's the bearded head. St Baaf (aka St Bavo) turns up again above the **high altar**, a marble extravaganza featuring the saint ascending to heaven on an untidy

The ornate pulpit at St-Baafskathedral

heap of clouds. Also in the north transept is the entrance to the dank and capacious **crypt**, a survivor from the earlier Romanesque church. The crypt is stuffed with religious bric-a-brac of only limited interest, the main exception being a superb triptych, *The Crucifixion of Christ*, by **Justus van Gent** (1410–80), who trained in Flanders but went on to live in Italy. This depicts the crucified Christ flanked, on the left, by Moses purifying the waters of Mara with wood, and to the right by Moses and the bronze serpent, which cured poisoned Israelites on sight. As the Bible has it: "So Moses made a bronze serpent [as the Lord had commanded] and set it on a pole; and if a serpent bit any man, he would look at the bronze serpent and live".

CityCard Gent

A bargain if you're set on seeing most of the sights, a **CityCard Gent** covers all of the key attractions, provides free and unlimited use of the city's buses and trams and includes a boat trip and a day's bike rental; it costs €30 for 48hr, €35 for 72hr. It's on sale at any of the participants as well as from tourist information (see page 145).

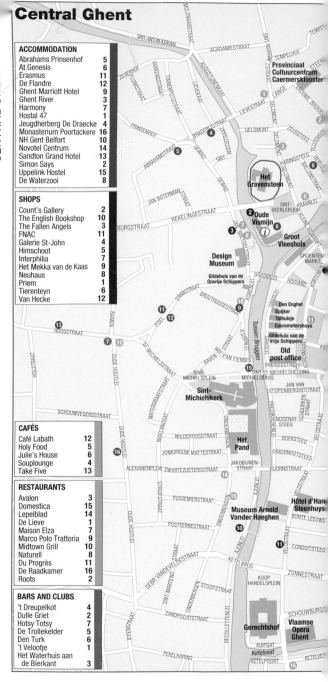

Central Ghent

ACCOMMODATION

Abrahams Prinsenhof	5
At Genesis	6
Erasmus	11
De Flandre	12
Ghent Marriott Hotel	9
Ghent River	3
Harmony	7
Hostal 47	1
Jeugdherberg De Draecke	4
Monasterium Poortackere	16
NH Gent Belfort	10
Novotel Centrum	14
Sandton Grand Hotel	13
Simon Says	2
Uppelink Hostel	15
De Waterzooi	8

SHOPS

Count's Gallery	2
The English Bookshop	10
The Fallen Angels	3
FNAC	11
Galerie St-John	4
Himschoot	5
Interphilia	7
Het Mekka van de Kaas	9
Neuhaus	8
Priem	1
Tierenteyn	6
Van Hecke	12

CAFÉS

Café Labath	12
Holy Food	5
Julie's House	6
Souplounge	4
Take Five	13

RESTAURANTS

Avalon	3
Domestica	15
Lepelblad	14
De Lieve	1
Maison Elza	7
Marco Polo Trattoria	9
Midtown Grill	10
Naturell	8
Du Progrès	11
De Raadkamer	16
Roots	2

BARS AND CLUBS

't Dreupelkot	4
Dulle Griet	2
Hotsy Totsy	7
De Trollekelder	5
Den Turk	6
't Velootje	1
Het Waterhuis aan de Bierkant	3

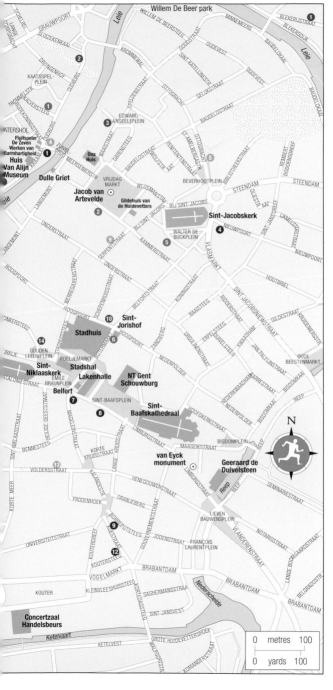

Willem De Beer park

BLEKERIJSTRAAT ❶
BLEKERSDIJK

MINNEMEERS

BAUDELOKAAL

Leie

GRAUWPOORT

WILLEM DE BEERSTEG

Leie

WILLEM DE BEERSTRAAT

GOUDSTRAAT

OUDEVEST

SLUIZEKENKAAL

KROMMEWAL

SINT-KATELIJNESTR

OUDEVEST

❷

DUDZELE

SPELDENSTRAAT

OTTOGRACHT

GELUKSTRAAT

BAUDELOSTRAAT

KAATSSPEL-PLEIN

DRONGENHOF

EDWARD
ANSEELEPLEIN

❸

GARENSTEEG

BAUDELOSTR AAT

SINT-AMELBERGA STR

PENITENTENSTRAAT

OTTOGRACHT

❺

BIBLIOTHEEKSTRAAT

REMBERT
DODOENSDREEF

TREMPELSTR.
KALVERSTEEG ❶

KONINGSTEEG

DUDZELE

WAASTRAAT

Ons
Huis

MEERSENIERSTR

BAUDELOSTR AAT

WIJZEMANSTRA

BEVERHOUTPLEIN

STEENDAM

STEENDAM

WATERSHOL

Fluitspeler
De Zeven
Werken van
Barmhartigheid
Huis
Van Alijn
Museum

❶ ❹ ZANDBRUG

VRIJDAG
MARKT

Jacob van
Artevelde ☉

Gildehuis van
de Huidevetters

QUISTI AAT

LIKMEESTERSTRAAT

ZANDBRUG

Dulle Griet

LANGEMUNT

❷

BIJ SINT-JACOBS

Sint-Jacobskerk

NIEUWPOORT

SINT-JANSDREEF

NIEUWPOORT

Leie

LANGEMUNT

ONDERSTRAAT

❾ SERPENTSTRAAT ❺

WALTER DE
BUCKPLEIN

KAMMERSTRAAT

VLASMARKT ❹

NIEUWPOORT

LANGEMUNT

WEBERSBRUGSTRAAT

ONDERSTRAAT

KONINGSTRAAT

HOUTBRIEI

HOOGPOORT

GROENEBRIERSTRAAT

BELFORTSTRAAT

BAARSTEEG

SINT-JACOBSNIEUWSTRAAT

GILDESTRAAT

KRUIDENIERSSTR

DONKERSTEEG

HOOGPOORT

❿ Sint-
Jorishof

HOOGPOORT

ZANDBERG

RIJZESTRAAT

ERPELSTEEG

DUIVEL STEEG

KWAANHAM

URSULINENSTRAAT

JAN PALFIJNSTRAAT

OUDE
BEESTENMARKT

GOUDEN
LEEUWPLEIN ⓮

IRKLE

Stadhuis

❻

Stadshal

POELJEMARKT

NEDERPOLDER

BISDOMKAAI

Sint-
Niklaaskerk

EMILE
BRAUNPLEIN

Lakenhale

NT Gent
Schouwburg

NEDERKWAADHAMKABRESTRAAT

NEDERPOLDER

BISDOMKAAI

REEP

Belfort

❼

SINT-BAAFSPLEIN

Sint-
Baafskathedraal

HOOFDKERKSTRAAT

NEDERPOLDER

❽

LIMBURGSTRAAT

MAGELEINSTRAAT

BENNESTEEG

HEILIGE GEESTSTRAAT

MAASEIKSTRAAT

BISDOMPLEIN

N

KORTE
KRUISSTRAAT

LANGE KRUISSTRAAT

van Eyck
monument ☉

Geeraard de
Duivelsteen

VOLDERSSTRAAT ⓭

KALANDEBERG

HENEGOUWENSTRAAT

LIMBURGSTRAAT

Reep

SEMINARIESTRAAT

PADDENHOEK

ORANJEBERG

LIEVEN
BAUWENSPLEIN

VLAANDERENSTRAAT

NOTARISSTRAAT

UNIVERSITEITSTRAAT

BORLUUTSTRAAT

KOUTERSTEEG

GOUDENLEEUWSTRAAT

JODENSTRAAT

FRANÇOIS
LAURENTPLEIN

LANGE BOOMGAARDSTRAAT

BELGRADOSTR.

KOUTERDREEF

❾

⓬

KOUTERSTRAAT

BRABANTDAM

BRABANTDAM

KOUTER

VOGELMARKT

KLEINVLEESHUISSTEEG

KORTEDAGSTEEG

SAGHERMANSSTRAAT

BRABANTDAM

Nederschelde

SINT-JANSVEST

Concertzaal
Handelsbeurs

GROTE HUIDEVETTERSHOEK

Ketelvaart

WALPOORTSTR

KETELVEST

KORIANDERSTRAAT

0	metres	100
0	yards	100

Stadhuis

Stadhuis, Ghent

MAP P.96, POCKET MAP C13

Botermarkt. Guided tours only: May–Sept
Mon–Fri (1 daily) as the first 45min of the
2hr walking tour organized by the Guides'
Association (see page 98). €10.

Stretching along the Botermarkt is
the striking **Stadhuis** (City Hall),
whose discordant facade comprises
two distinct sections. The later
section, framing the central stairway,
dates from the 1580s and offers a
fine example of Italian Renaissance
architecture, its crisp symmetries
faced by a multitude of black-
painted pilasters. In stark contrast
are the wild, curling patterns of the
section to the immediate north,
carved in Flamboyant Gothic style
at the beginning of the sixteenth
century to a design by the celebrated
architect, **Rombout Keldermans**
(1460–1531). The whole of the
Stadhuis was to have been built by
Keldermans, but the money ran
out and the city couldn't afford
to finish it off until much later –
hence today's mixture of styles.
Look carefully at Keldermans'
work and you'll spot all sorts of
charming details, especially in the
elaborate tracery, decorated with
oak leaves and acorns as well as
vines laden with grapes, though the
statuettes in the niches, representing
important historical personages in
characteristic poses, were only added
in the nineteenth century.

Guided tours of the Stadhuis
amble round a series of halls and
chambers, the most interesting
being the old Court of Justice
or **Pacificatiezaal** (Pacification
Hall), where the Pacification
of Ghent was signed in 1576.
A plaque commemorates this
treaty, which momentarily
bound the rebel armies of the
Low Countries (today's Belgium
and the Netherlands) together
against their rulers, the Spanish
Habsburgs. The carrot offered by
the dominant Protestants was the
promise of religious freedom, but
they failed to deliver and much of
the south (present-day Belgium)
soon returned to the Spanish fold.
The hall's charcoal-and-cream
tiled floor is designed in the form
of a maze. No one's quite certain
why, but it's thought that more
privileged felons (or sinners) had to
struggle round the maze on their

Guided walking tours

Guided walking tours are popular in Ghent. The standard
tour, operated by city's Guides' Association, is a two-hour jaunt
around the city centre (May–Sept 1 daily, Oct–March Sat & Sun 1
daily; tours start at 2pm; €10); these include a visit to either the
Stadhuis (Mon–Fri) or the Cathedral (Sat & Sun). Tickets are on
sale at tourist information (see page 145) and advance booking –
at least a few hours ahead of time – is strongly recommended.

knees as a substitute punishment for a pilgrimage to Jerusalem – a good deal if ever there was one.

Lakenhalle

MAP P.96, POCKET MAP C13
Botermarkt. No public access except to the attached Belfort (see page 99)

The conspicuous **Lakenhalle** is a hunk of a building with an unhappy history. Work began on the hall in the early fifteenth century, but the cloth trade collapsed before it was finished and it was only grudgingly completed in 1903. Since then, no one has ever quite worked out what to do with it and today the building is little more than an empty shell, though the basement did once hold the municipal prison, whose entrance was on the west side of the building through the **Mammelokker** (The Suckling), a grandiose Louis XIV-style portal of 1741. Part gateway and part warder's lodging, the Mammelokker displays a sculpture illustrating the classical legend of Cimon, whom the Romans condemned to death by starvation; his daughter, Pero, saved the day by suckling him – hence the name.

The Belfort at the Lakenhalle

Belfort, Ghent

MAP P.96, POCKET MAP C13
Botermarkt ☎ 09 233 39 54, ⊕ belfortgent. be. Daily 10am–6pm. €8.

The first-floor entrance on the south side of the Lakenhalle is the only way to reach the **Belfort** (Belfry), a much-amended medieval edifice whose soaring spire is topped by a corpulent gilded copper dragon. Once a watchtower and storehouse, the interior is now largely empty except for a few old bells and incidental statues alongside the rusting remains of a brace of antique dragons, which formerly perched on top of the spire. The belfry is equipped with a **glass-sided lift** that climbs up to the roof, where consolation is provided in the form of excellent views over the city centre.

St-Niklaaskerk

MAP P.96, POCKET MAP C13
Cataloniestraat ☎ 09 234 28 69, ⊕ visit. gent.be. April–Sept Mon 2–5pm, Tues–Sun 10am–5pm; Oct–March daily 2–5pm. Free.

An architectural hybrid dating from the thirteenth century, **St-Niklaaskerk** is a handsome affair, its arching buttresses and

CENTRAL GHENT

Boat trips

Throughout the season, **boat trips** explore Ghent's inner waterways, departing from the Korenlei quay, just near the Korenmarkt, and from the Vleeshuisbrug, beside the Kraanlei (April–Oct daily 10am–6pm; €8). Trips last about forty minutes and leave every fifteen minutes or so, though the wait can be longer as boats often delay their departure until they are reasonably full. Queues are commonplace at the height of the season, especially on the weekend.

pencil-thin turrets elegantly attenuating the lines of the nave, in a classic example of the early Scheldt Gothic. Inside, many of the Baroque furnishings and fittings have been removed and the windows un-bricked, thus returning the church to its early – and lighter – appearance. The highlight is the giant-sized Baroque **high altar** with its mammoth God the Father glowering down its back, blowing the hot wind of the Last Judgement from his mouth and surrounded by a flock of cherubs. The church is sometimes used for temporary art exhibitions.

St-Niklaaskerk

Korenmarkt

MAP P.96, POCKET MAP C13

St-Niklaaskerk marks the southern end of the **Korenmarkt** (Corn Market), the traditional focus of the city, comprising a long and wide cobbled area where the grain that once kept the city fed was traded after it was unloaded from the boats that anchored on the Graslei dock nearby (see page 102). The one noteworthy building is the former **post office**, now a shopping mall, whose combination of Gothic Revival and neo-Renaissance styles illustrates the eclecticism popular in Belgium at the beginning of the twentieth century. The carved heads encircling the building represent the great and the good, who came to the city for the Great Exhibition of 1913, including – curiously enough – Florence Nightingale.

St-Michielsbrug

MAP P.96, POCKET MAP B13

Behind the old post office, **St-Michielsbrug** (St Michael's bridge) offers fine views back over the towers and turrets that pierce the Ghent skyline. This is no accident: the bridge was built in 1913 to provide visitors to the Great Exhibition with a vantage point from which to admire the city centre. The bridge also overlooks the city's oldest harbour, the **Tussen Bruggen** (Between the Bridges), from whose quays boats leave for trips around the canals (see box above).

St-Michielsbrug

St-Michielskerk

MAP P.96, POCKET MAP B13
St-Michielsplein ☎ **09 234 28 69,** Ⓦ **visit.**
gent.be. April–Sept Mon–Sat 2–5pm. Free.
Beside St-Michielsbrug rises the
bulky mass of **St-Michielskerk**,
a heavy-duty Gothic structure
begun in the 1440s. The city's
Protestants seem to have taken a
particularly strong disliking to the
place, ransacking it twice – once in
1566 and again in 1579 – and the
repairs were never quite finished, as
witnessed by the clumsily truncated
tower. The interior is a surprisingly
handsome affair, the broad sweep
of the five-aisled nave punctuated
by tall and slender columns that
shoot up to the arching vaults of
the roof. Most of the furnishings
and fittings are Gothic Revival, but
they are enlivened by a scattering
of sixteenth- and seventeenth-
century paintings, the pick of
which is a splendidly impassioned
Crucifixion by **Anthony van
Dyck** (1599–1641) displayed in
the north transept. Trained in
Antwerp, where he worked in
Rubens' workshop, van Dyck made
extended visits to England and Italy
in the 1620s, before returning to

Markets

Ghent does a good line in open-air **markets**. There's a large and
popular flea market (**prondelmarkt**) on Bij St Jacobs and adjoining
Beverhoutplein (Fri, Sat & Sun 8am–1pm), where you can pick
up any and everything from a pair of old cords to a well-worn
statuette of a saint; an extensive Sunday morning flower market
on the Kouter, on the south side of the centre, just off Veldstraat
(7am–1pm); organic foodstuffs on the Groentenmarkt (Fri
7.30am–1pm); a weekly second-hand book market on the Ajuinlei
(Sun 8am–1pm); a weekend craft and bygones market on the
Groentenmarkt (Sat & Sun 7.30am–1pm); and a bird market (not
for the squeamish) on the Vrijdagmarkt on Sundays (7am–1pm).

The doorway to one of the guild houses of the Graslei

Antwerp in 1628. He stayed there for four years – during which time he painted this *Crucifixion* – before migrating to England to become portrait painter to Charles I and his court, dying in London just before the outbreak of the English Civil War.

Graslei

MAP P.96, POCKET MAP B13

Ghent's boatmen and grainweighers were crucial to the functioning of the medieval city, and they built a row of splendid **guild houses** along the **Graslei**, each gable decorated with an appropriate sign or symbol. Working your way north from St-Michielsbrug, the first building of distinction is the **Gildehuis van de Vrije Schippers** (Guild House of the Free Boatmen), at no. 14, where the badly weathered sandstone is decorated with scenes of boatmen weighing anchor, plus a delicate carving of a caravel – the type of Mediterranean sailing ship used by Columbus – located above the door. Medieval Ghent had **two boatmen guilds** – the Free, who could discharge their cargoes within the city, and the Unfree,

who were obliged to unload their goods into the vessels of the **Free Boatmen** at the edge of the city in an arrangement typical of the complex regulations governing the guilds.

Next door, at nos. 12–13, the seventeenth-century **Cooremetershuys** (Corn Measurers' House) was where city officials weighed and graded corn behind a facade graced by cartouches and garlands of fruit. Next to this, at no. 11, stands the quaint **Tolhuisje**, another delightful example of Flemish Renaissance architecture, built to house the customs officers in 1698, while the adjacent limestone **Spijker** (Staple House), at no. 10, boasts a surly Romanesque facade dating from around 1200. It was here that the city stored its grain supply for over five hundred years until a fire gutted the interior. Finally, two doors down at no. 8, the splendid **Den Enghel** is named after the banner-bearing angel that decorates the facade; the building was originally the stonemasons' guild house, as evidenced by the effigies of the four Roman martyrs who were the guild's patron saints, though they are depicted in medieval attire rather than togas and sandals.

The Groentenmarkt

MAP P.96, POCKET MAP C12

Just north of Graslei is the **Groentenmarkt** (Vegetable Market), where a jangle of old buildings includes one especially distinctive shop, Tierenteyn, the mustard specialist (see page 113). The west side of the square is flanked by a long line of stone gables which once enclosed the **Groot Vleeshuis** (Great Butchers' Hall), a covered market where meat was sold under the careful control of the city council – the private sale of meat was forbidden in medieval Ghent. The gables date from the fifteenth century and could do with a brush-up and the interior, with its intricate wooden roof, now holds a delicatessen.

The Korenlei

MAP P.96, POCKET MAP B13

Across the Grasbrug bridge from the Graslei lies the **Korenlei**, which trips along the western side of the old city harbour. Unlike the Graslei opposite, none of the medieval buildings have survived here and instead there's a series of expansive, high-gabled Neoclassical merchants' houses, mostly dating from the eighteenth century. It's the general ensemble that appeals rather than any particular building, but the **Gildehuis van de Onvrije Schippers** (Guild House of the Unfree Boatmen), at no.7, does boast a fetching eighteenth-century facade decorated with whimsical dolphins and bewigged lions, all bulging eyes and rows of teeth.

Design Museum

MAP P.96, POCKET MAP B12

Jan Breydelstraat 5. Mon & Tues, Thurs & Fri 9.30am–5.30pm; Sat & Sun 10am–6pm; closed Wed. €10. ☎ 09 267 99 99, ⓦ designmuseumgent.be

The enjoyable **Design Museum** focuses on Belgian decorative and applied arts, with the wide-ranging collection divided into two distinct sections. At the front, squeezed into what was once an eighteenth-century patrician's mansion, is an attractive sequence of **period rooms**, mostly illustrating the Baroque and the Rococo. The original dining room is especially fine, from its fancy painted ceiling, ornate chandelier and Chinese porcelain through to its intricately carved elm panelling. The second section, at the back of the mansion, comprises a **modern display** area used both for temporary exhibitions and to showcase the museum's collection of applied arts, dating from 1880 onwards. Here, the Art Nouveau material is the most visually arresting, especially the finely crafted furnishings of **Henry van der Velde** (1863–1957).

St-Veerleplein

MAP P.96, POCKET MAP B12

Public punishments ordered by the counts and countesses of Flanders were carried out in front of the castle on **St-Veerleplein**,

Merchants' houses on the Korenlei

now an attractive cobbled square with an ersatz punishment post plonked here in 1913 and topped off by a lion carrying the banner of Flanders. In case the citizenry became indifferent to beheading, it was here also that currency counterfeiters were thrown into boiling oil or water.

Oude Vismijn

MAP P.96, POCKET MAP B12
St-Veerleplein.

Standing proud at the back of St-Veerleplein, beside the junction of the city's two main canals, is the Baroque facade of the **Oude Vismijn** (Old Fish Market), which features Neptune on a chariot drawn by sea horses. To either side are allegorical figures representing the River Leie (Venus) and the River Scheldt (Hercules), the two rivers that spawned the city. After years of neglect, the Oude Vismijn has been redeveloped and is now home to the tourist office (see page 145).

Het Gravensteen

MAP P.96, POCKET MAP B12
St-Veerleplein ☏ 09 225 93 06,
ⓦ gravensteen.stad.gent. Daily: April–Oct

10am–6pm; Nov–March 9am–5pm. €10.
The cold, forbidding walls and unyielding turrets of **Het Gravensteen**, the castle of the counts of Flanders, look sinister enough to have been lifted from a Bosch painting. They were first raised in 1180 as much to intimidate the town's unruly citizens as to protect them, and, considering the castle has been used for all sorts of purposes since then (even a cotton mill), it has survived in remarkably good nick. The imposing **gateway** comprises a deep-arched, heavily fortified tunnel leading to a large **courtyard**, which is framed by protective battlements complete with ancient arrow slits and apertures for boiling oil and water. Overlooking the courtyard are the castle's two main buildings: the **count's residence** on the left and the **keep** on the right, the latter riddled with narrow, interconnected staircases set within the thickness of the walls. A **self-guided tour** takes you through this labyrinth, the first highlight being a room full of medieval military hardware, from suits of armour, pikes, swords, daggers and early pistols through

Het Gravensteen

to a pair of exquisitely crafted sixteenth-century crossbows. Beyond is a gruesome collection of instruments of torture; a particularly dank, underground dungeon (or *oubliette*); and the counts' vaulted session room – or council chamber. It's also possible to walk along most of the castle's encircling wall, from where there are pleasing views over the city centre.

Kraanlei

MAP P.96, POCKET MAP C12

The **Kraanlei** cuts an attractive course along the canalized River Leie, passing the Huis van Alijn Museum (see page 106) before encountering two especially fine facades. First up, at no.79, is **De Zeven Werken van Barmhartigheid** (The Seven Works of Mercy), which takes its name from the miniature panels which decorate its front. The panels on the top level, from left to right, illustrate the mercies of visiting the sick, ministering to prisoners and burying the dead, whilst those below (again from left to right) show feeding the hungry, providing water for the thirsty, and clothing the naked. The seventh good work – giving shelter to the stranger – was provided inside the building, which was once an inn, so, perhaps rather too subtly, there's no decorative panel. The adjacent **Fluitspeler** (The Flautist), the corner house at no. 81, dates from 1669 and is now occupied by a restaurant. The six bas-relief terracotta panels on this facade sport allegorical representations of the five senses plus a flying deer; above, on the cornice, are the figures of Faith, Hope and Charity.

Patershol

MAP P.96, POCKET MAP C12

Behind Kraanlei are the lanes and alleys of the **Patershol**, a tight web of brick terraced houses dating from the seventeenth century. Once the heart of the Flemish

The Fluitspeler on the Kraanlei

working-class city, the Patershol hid the skids in the 1890s when industry moved to the outskirts of town, leaving a district known for its drinking dens and down-at-heel lodgings. By the 1970s, the Patershol had become a slum threatened with demolition, but, after much debate, the area was saved from the developers and a process of restoration begun, the result being today's modernised terrace houses and apartments. The process is still under way and the fringes of the Patershol remain a ragbag of decay and restoration, but it's still one of Ghent's most diverting districts with one specific sight: the Provinciaal Cultuurcentrum Caermersklooster.

Provinciaal Cultuurcentrum Caermersklooster

MAP P.96, POCKET MAP C11
Lange Steenstraat 14 ☎ 09 269 29 10, ⓦ caermersklooster.be. Thurs–Sun 10am–5pm. Entrance fee varies with exhibition.
The capacious former Carmelite Monastery on the edge of the Patershol has been turned into the **Provinciaal Cultuurcentrum**

Exhibition at Huis van Alijn Museum

Caermersklooster, which offers an ambitious programme of temporary exhibitions. There is space for two or three exhibitions at any one time and they mix things up with contemporary art, photography, design and fashion displayed alongside more socially engaged exhibitions – with one recent highlight being an immaculately researched feature on "Poverty in Belgium".

Huis van Alijn Museum

MAP P.96, POCKET MAP C12
Kraanlei 65 ☏ 09 235 38 00,
ⓦ huisvanalijn.be. Mon & Tues, Thurs & Fri 9am–5pm; Sat & Sun 10am–6pm; closed Wed. €6.

The **Huis van Alijn** folklore museum occupies a series of pretty little almshouses set around a central courtyard. Dating from the fourteenth century, the almshouses were built following a major scandal reminiscent of *Romeo and Juliet*. In 1354, two members of the Rijms family murdered three of the rival Alijns when they were at Mass in St-Baafskathedraal. The immediate cause of the affray was jealousy – one man from each clan was after the same woman – but the dispute went deeper, reflecting the commercial animosity of two guilds, the weavers and the fullers. The murderers fled for their lives and were condemned to death in absentia, but were eventually – eight years later – pardoned on condition that they paid for the construction of a set of almshouses, which was to be named after the victims. The result was the Huis van Alijn, which became a hospice for elderly women and then a workers' tenement until the city council snapped it up in the 1940s.

The **museum** consists of two sets of rooms, either side of the courtyard, depicting local life and work in the nineteenth and twentieth centuries. The duller rooms hold reconstructed shops and workshops – a dispensary, a cobbler's and so forth – the more interesting are thematic, illustrating particular aspects of traditional Flemish society, popular entertainment for example. The more substantial exhibits are explained in multilingual leaflets, which are available in the appropriate room, but generally the labelling is very skimpy. One of the rooms on the right-hand side of the museum has a bank of miniature TV screens showing short, locally-made amateur films in a continuous cycle. Some of these date back to the 1920s, but most are post-war including a snippet featuring a local 1970s soccer team in terrifyingly tight shorts. Overlooking the central courtyard in between the two sets of rooms is the **chapel**, a pleasantly gaudy affair built in the 1540s and now decorated with folksy shrines and votive offerings. When they aren't out on loan, the chapel is also home to a pair of "goliaths", large and fancily dressed wooden figures that are a common feature of Belgian street processions and festivals.

Dulle Griet

MAP P.96, POCKET MAP C12

From the Kraanlei, an antiquated little bridge leads over to **Dulle Griet** (Mad Meg), a lugubrious fifteenth-century **cannon** whose failure to fire provoked a bitter row between Ghent and the nearby Flemish town of Oudenaarde, where it was cast. In the 1570s, fearful of a Habsburg attack, Ghent purchased the **cannon** from Oudenaarde. As the region's most powerful siege gun, able to propel a 340kg cannonball several hundred metres, it seemed a good buy, but when Ghent's gunners tried it out, the barrel cracked on first firing and, much to the chagrin of Ghent's city council, Oudenaarde refused to offer a refund. The useless lump was then rolled to the edge of the Vrijdagmarkt, where it has stayed ever since.

Vrijdagmarkt

MAP P.96, POCKET MAP C12

A wide and open square, the **Vrijdagmarkt** was long the political centre of Ghent, the site of both public meetings and executions – sometimes at the same time. In the middle of the square stands a nineteenth-century statue of the guild leader **Jacob van Artevelde** (see page 108), portrayed addressing the people in heroic style. Of the buildings flanking the Vrijdagmarkt, the most appealing is the former **Gildehuis van de Huidevetters** (Tanners' Guild House), at no.37, a tall, Gothic structure whose stepped gables culminate in a dainty and distinctive corner turret – the Toreken. Also worth a second glance is the old headquarters of the trade unions, the **Ons Huis** (Our House), a sterling edifice built in eclectic style at the turn of the twentieth century.

Bij St-Jacobs

MAP P.96, POCKET MAP D12
St-Jacobskerk Bij St-Jacobs ☎ 09 223 25 26, Ⓦ visit.gent.be. April–Oct Fri & Sat 9.30am–12.30pm. Free.

Adjoining the Vrijdagmarkt is **Bij St-Jacobs**, a sprawling and irregularly shaped square whose centrepiece is the whopping **St-Jacobskerk**, a glum-looking edifice

Dulle Griet

Jacob van Artevelde comes to a sticky end

One of the most powerful of Ghent's medieval leaders, **Jacob van Artevelde** (1290–1345) was elected captain of all the guilds in 1337. Initially, he steered a delicate course during the interminable wars between France and England, keeping the city neutral – and the textile industry going – despite the machinations of both warring countries. Ultimately, however, he was forced to take sides, plumping for England. This proved his undoing: in a burst of Anglomania, Artevelde rashly suggested that a son of Edward III of England become the new Count of Flanders, an unpopular notion that prompted a mob to storm his house and hack him to death.

that partly dates from the twelfth century, its proudest features being its twin west towers and central spire. Inside, the heavily vaulted nave is awash with Baroque decoration from the gaudy pulpit to the kitsch high altar. The square hosts the city's biggest and best **flea market** (*prondelmarkt*; Fri–Sun 8am–1pm).

St-Jorishof

MAP P.96, POCKET MAP C13
Corner Botermarkt and Hoogpoort.
Facing the Stadhuis, **St-Jorishof** is one of the city's oldest buildings, its heavy-duty stonework dating from the fifteenth century. This was once the home of the Crossbowmen's Guild, and although the crossbow was a dead military duck by the time it was built, the guild was still a powerful political force – and long remained so. It was here, in 1477, that Mary of Burgundy (see page 55) was pressured into signing the Great Privilege confirming the city's commercial freedoms. Beyond St Jorishof, lining up along **Hoogpoort**, are some of the oldest facades in Ghent, sturdy if sometimes sooty Gothic structures also dating from the fifteenth century.

Geeraard de Duivelsteen

MAP P.96, POCKET MAP D14
Reep. No admission.

The forbidding **Geeraard de Duivelsteen** is a fortified palace of splendid Romanesque design built of grey limestone in the thirteenth century. The stronghold takes its name from Geeraard Vilain, who earned the soubriquet "duivel" (devil) for his acts of cruelty. Medieval Ghent was dotted with fortified houses (*stenen*) like this one, reflecting the fear the privileged few had of the rebellious guildsmen. The last noble moved out of the Duivelsteen in about 1350 and since then the building has been put to a bewildering range of uses, but today it stands empty.

Lieven Bauwensplein

MAP P.96, POCKET MAP D14
Across from the Duivelsteen is **Lieven Bauwensplein**, a square that takes its name from – and has a statue of – the local entrepreneur who founded the city's machine-manufactured textile industry. Born in 1769, Bauwens was an intrepid soul, who posed as an ordinary textile worker in England to learn how its (more technologically advanced) machinery worked. In the 1790s, he managed to smuggle a spinning jenny over to the continent and soon opened cotton mills in Ghent. It didn't, however, do Bauwens much good: he over-borrowed, his factories went bust and he died in poverty.

Van Eyck monument

MAP P.96, POCKET MAP D14
Limburgstraat.

In the shadow of the Cathedral, the **Van Eyck monument** celebrates the Eyck brothers, Hubert and Jan, the painter(s) of the *Adoration of the Mystic Lamb* (see page 110). The monument is a stodgy affair, knocked up for the Great Exhibition of 1913, but it's an interesting piece of art propaganda, proclaiming Hubert as co-painter of the altarpiece, when this is very speculative. Open on Hubert's knees is the *Book of Revelation*, which may or may not have given him artistic inspiration.

Veldstraat

MAP P.96, POCKET MAP B14–C13
Museum Arnold Vander Haeghen, Veldstraat 82 & Hôtel d'Hane-Steenhuyse, Veldstraat 55 ☎ 09 210 10 75, ⓦ visit.gent. be. Guided tours by prior arrangement: Thurs–Sat 2.30–4pm. €6 for the two.

The city's main shopping street, **Veldstraat**, leads south from the Korenmarkt, running parallel to the River Leie. By and large, it's a fairly ordinary strip, but the eighteenth-century mansion at no.82 holds the mildly diverting **Museum Arnold Vander Haeghen**, where pride of place goes to the Chinese salon, whose original silk wallpaper has survived intact. The Duke of Wellington stayed here in 1815 after the Battle of Waterloo, popping across the street to the **Hôtel d'Hane-Steenhuyse**, at no.55, to bolster the morale of the refugee King of France, Louis XVIII. Dating to 1768, the grand facade of Louis's hideaway has survived in good condition, its elaborate pediment sporting allegorical representations of Time and History – and tours of the interior amble round a series of expansive salons. Nearby rise a matching pair of grand, Neoclassical nineteenth-century buildings. On the right-hand side is the **Gerechtshof** (Law Courts), whose colossal pediment sports a frieze with the figure of Justice in the middle, the accused to one side and the condemned on the other. Opposite stands **Opera Ghent** – home to De Vlaamse Opera (see page 147) – whose facade is awash with playfully decorative stone panels.

Geeraard de Duivelsteen

The Adoration of the Mystic Lamb

In a side-chapel to the left of the cathedral entrance is Ghent's greatest treasure, a winged altarpiece known as *The Adoration of the Mystic Lamb* (*De Aanbidding van het Lam Gods*), a seminal work of the early 1430s, though of dubious provenance. Since the discovery of a Latin verse on its frame in the nineteenth century, academics have been arguing about who actually painted it. The inscription reads that **Hubert van Eyck** "than whom none was greater" began, and **Jan van Eyck**, "second in art", completed the work, but as nothing else is known of Hubert, some art historians doubt his existence. They argue that Jan, who lived and worked in several cities, including Ghent, was responsible for the painting and that only later, after Jan had firmly rooted himself in the rival city of Bruges, did the citizens of Ghent invent "Hubert" to counter his fame. No one knows for sure, but what is certain is that the artist (or artists) was able to capture a needle-sharp, luminous realism that must have stunned his contemporaries and remains a marvel today.

The cover screens

At the back of the altarpiece, the **cover screens** hold a beautiful Annunciation scene with the archangel Gabriel's wings reaching up to the timbered ceiling of a Flemish house. The shadows of the angel dapple the room, emphasizing the reality of the apparition – a technique repeated on the opposite cover panel around the figure of Mary. Below, the donor, Joos Vydt – one-time city mayor and merchant – and his wife Isabella Borlout kneel piously alongside statues of the saints.

The upper level

By design, the restrained exterior was but a foretaste of what lay within – a striking, visionary work of art whose brilliant colours and precise draughtsmanship still takes the breath away. On the **upper level** sit God the Father (some say Christ Triumphant), the Virgin and John the Baptist in gleaming clarity; to the right are musician-angels and a nude, pregnant Eve; and on the left is Adam plus a group of singing angels, who strain to read their music.

The lower central panel

In the **lower central panel** the Lamb, the symbol of Christ's sacrifice, is depicted in a heavenly paradise. The Lamb stands on an altar whose rim is minutely inscribed with a quotation from the Gospel of St John, "Behold the Lamb of God, which taketh away the sins of the world" – and hence the wound in the lamb from which blood issues into a gold cup. Four groups of religious figures converge on the Lamb from the corners of the central panel.

The side panels

On the **side panels**, approaching the Lamb across symbolically rough and stony ground, are more saintly figures. On the right, there are two groups: St Anthony with his hermits and St Christopher, shown here as a giant with a band of pilgrims. On the left side panel come the horsemen, the inner group symbolizing the Warriors of Christ – including St George bearing a shield with a red cross – and the outer the **Just Judges**, a replica panel in which the figures sport fancy Flemish attire.

Scares and alarms

The **Just Judges panel** was added during the 1950s to replace the original, which was stolen in 1934 and never recovered. The lost panel features in **Albert Camus**'s novel *The Fall*, whose protagonist keeps it in a cupboard, declining to return it. There has been endless speculation as to who stole the panel and why. Some argue that the Nazis orchestrated the theft, but suspicion ultimately rested on **Arsène Goedertier**, a local stockbroker and conservative politician, who made a deathbed confession.

The theft was just one of many **dramatic events** to befall the painting – indeed, it's remarkable that the altarpiece has survived at all. The Calvinists wanted to destroy it; Philip II of Spain tried to acquire it; the Emperor Joseph II disapproved of the painting so violently that he replaced the nude Adam and Eve with a clothed version of 1784 (exhibited today on a column at the start of the nave just inside the cathedral entrance); and, near the end of World War II, the Germans hid it in an Austrian salt mine, where it remained until American soldiers rescued it in 1945.

Galerie St-John

Shops

Count's Gallery

MAP P.96, POCKET MAP B12
Rekelingestraat 1 ☏ 09 225 31 27.
Wed–Sun 10am–6pm.

This idiosyncratic little shop, just
opposite Het Gravensteen, sells
an eclectic range of souvenirs,
miniature models, postcards and so
forth – great for kitsch gifts.

The English Bookshop

MAP P.96, POCKET MAP B14
Ajuinlei 15 ☏ 09 223 02 36. Mon–Sat
11am–6pm.

Small, but well-stocked secondhand
bookstore selling all sorts of cheap
English-language books, particularly
on historical and military subjects.
Spreads over two dense floors.

The Fallen Angels

MAP P.96, POCKET MAP B12
Jan Breydelstraat 29–31 ☏ 09 223 94 15,
ⓦ the-fallen-angels.com. Ganesha's shop:
Mon–Sat except Wed 11am–noon & 1–6pm;
Wed 1–6pm; Isabella's shop: Wed–Sat
1.30–5.30pm.

Mother and daughter run these two
adjacent shops, selling all manner

of antique bric-a-brac, from
postcards, posters and religious
images through to teddy bears and
toys. Intriguing at best, twee at
worst, but a distinctive source of
unusual gifts nonetheless.

FNAC

MAP P.96, POCKET MAP B14
Veldstraat 88 ☏ 09 223 40 80, ⓦ fnac.be.
Mon–Sat 10am–6.30pm.

Mixed bag of a chain store,
whose several floors sell electrical
appliances, cameras, TVs and all
sorts of gadgets. Also has a modest
selection of English-language
books, mostly fiction, and a wide
range of road, cycling and hiking
maps with good coverage of
Belgium. Sells tickets for many
mainstream cultural events too.

Galerie St-John

MAP P.96, POCKET MAP D12
Nieuwpoort 2 ☏ 09 225 82 62, ⓦ st-john.
be. Mon–Thurs 2–6pm, Fri & Sat 10am–
noon & 2–6pm, Sun 10am–noon.

Arguably the best antique shop in
Ghent – and there is competition –
this well-regarded place specializes in
nineteenth- and twentieth-century
fine and applied art, everything from

silverware and furniture through to chandeliers, ceramics, glass, crystal and oil paintings.

Himschoot

MAP P.96, POCKET MAP C12
Groentenmarkt 1 ☏ 0486 37 59 26, ⓦ bakkerijhimschoot.be. Daily 8am–6.30pm.
Traditional bakery, where the bread is baked in the basement before being packed tight into the shelves of the shop above. Over sixty different sorts of bread, plus tasty tarts, cakes and scones – all at bargain prices. No wonder there are queues at peak times.

Interphilia

MAP P.96, POCKET MAP C13
St-Baafsplein 4 ☏ 09 225 46 80, ⓦ interphila.be. Mon–Sat 10am–noon & 1–5.30pm.
Temptingly old-fashioned stamp and coin shop, where every nook and cranny is stuffed to the gills. Also sells antique postcards, vintage badges, posters and insignia.

Het Mekka van de Kaas

MAP P.96, POCKET MAP C13
Koestraat 9 ☏ 09 225 83 66, ⓦ hetmekkavandekaas.be. Tues–Fri 9am–1pm & 1.30–6.30pm, Sat 9am–6.30pm.
Literally the "Cheese Mecca", this small specialist cheese shop offers a remarkable range of traditional and exotic cheeses – try some of the delicious Ghent goats' cheese (*geitenkaas*). Sells a good range of wine, too.

Neuhaus

MAP P.96, POCKET MAP C14
St-Baafsplein 20 ☏ 09 223 43 74, ⓦ neuhauschocolates.com. Mon–Sat 10am–6pm.
Probably Belgium's best chocolate chain, with mouthwatering chocolates at €18 for 250g – you can go cheaper, but not better. Try their Manons, stuffed white chocolates, which come with fresh cream, vanilla and coffee fillings, or the Caprices – pralines stuffed

with crispy nougat, fresh cream and soft-centred chocolate. Two stores in Ghent – and this is the more central.

Priem

MAP P.96, POCKET MAP C12
Zuivelbrugstraat 1 ☏ 09 223 25 37. Mon 2–5.30pm, Tues–Fri 9.30am–12.30pm & 2–6pm, Sat 9.30am–12.30pm & 2–5.30pm.
One of the oddest shops in Ghent, *Priem* has an extraordinary range of vintage wallpaper dating from the 1950s. Zuivelbrugstraat is the location of the main shop, but there are three other neighbouring premises on the Kraanlei.

Tierenteyn

MAP P.96, POCKET MAP C12
Groentenmarkt 3 ☏ 09 225 83 36, ⓦ tierenteyn-verlent.be. Mon 10am–6pm, Tues–Fri 9am–6pm, Sat 9.30am–6pm.
This traditional shop, one of the city's most delightful, makes its own mustards – wonderful, tongue-tickling stuff displayed in shelf upon shelf of ceramic and glass jars. A small jar will set you back about €5.

Van Hecke

MAP P.96, POCKET MAP C14
Koestraat 42 ☏ 09 225 43 57, ⓦ chocolaterievanhecke.be. Tues–Sat 9am–6pm, Sun 9am–1pm.

Tierenteyn

Many locals swear that this independent chocolatier sells the best chocolates and cakes in town. Mouthwatering, lip-smacking, taste-bud satisfying stuff. Established in the 1930s – and in the same family for four generations.

Cafés

Café Labath

MAP P.96, POCKET MAP A13
Oude Houtlei 1 ☎ 0476 99 42 81,
ⓦ cafelabath.be. Mon–Fri 8am–7pm, Sat 9am–7pm, Sun 10am–6pm.
Specialist coffee house in neat, modern premises that makes much of the quality of its beans – with good reason. Try the Java or the Ethiopian. Sells snacks, soups and teas too. Attracts a boho, avant-garde crew.

Holy Food

MAP P.96, POCKET MAP D12
Beverhoutplein 15 ⓦ holyfoodmarket.be.
Daily 11am–10pm.
A deconsecrated old church has been turned into this multi-outlet, indoor food (and drink) market – sit down or takeaway. There is not

Café Labath

much finesse to the food, but lots of choice, anything from Malay street food to Portuguese tapas.

Julie's House

MAP P.96, POCKET MAP C12
Kraanlei 13 ☎ 09 233 33 90, ⓦ julieshouse.be. Wed–Sun 9am–6pm.
"Baked with love, served with joy" is the boast here – it's a little OTT perhaps, but *Julie's* home-made cakes and patisseries are truly delicious. They also serve breakfasts (till 2pm) and pancakes. Squeezed into an ancient and somewhat rickety terrace house in one of the prettiest parts of the city.

Souplounge

MAP P.96, POCKET MAP C12
Zuivelbrugstraat 4, just off Vrijdagmarkt
☎ 09 223 62 03, ⓦ souplounge.be. Daily 10am–7pm.
Bright and cheerful self-service café, where the big bowls of freshly made soup are the main event – from just €5. Filling sandwiches and salads too.

Take Five

MAP P.96, POCKET MAP C14
Voldersstraat 10 ☎ 09 311 44 96, ⓦ take-five-espressobar.be. Mon–Fri 8am–6pm & Sat 9am–6pm.
Bright and brisk coffee bar with a cool sound track – jazz meets house – and pleasing modern decor. Offers a great range of specialist-bean coffees, plus a selection of teas and delicious cakes and pastries.

Restaurants

Avalon

MAP P.96, POCKET MAP B12
Geldmunt 32 ☎ 09 224 37 24, ⓦ restaurantavalon.be. Tues–Sat 11.30am–2.30pm.
This long-established vegetarian restaurant offers a wide range of well-prepared dishes – be sure to look out for the daily specials, which cost a bargain €18. Local, seasonal produce takes centre stage.

Choose from one of the many different rooms or the terrace at the back in the summer.

Domestica

MAP P.96, POCKET MAP B14
Onderbergen 27 ☎ 09 223 53 00,
🌐 domestica.be. Mon 6.30–10pm,
Tues–Fri noon–2pm & 6.30–10.30pm, Sat
6.30–10.30pm.

Smart and chic brasserie-restaurant serving up an excellent range of Belgian dishes – both French and Flemish – in nouvelle cuisine style. Has a garden terrace for good-weather eating. Main courses from €28.

Lepelblad

MAP P.96, POCKET MAP B14
Onderbergen 40 ☎ 09 324 02 44,
🌐 lepelblad.be. Tues 5.30–11pm, Wed–Sat
noon–3pm & 5.30–11pm.

Extremely popular restaurant, with a heaving pavement terrace, where the ever-changing menu is inventive and creative with pasta dishes, salads and traditional Flemish cuisine to the fore – try, for example, the Ghent waterzooi (€22). The arty decor is good fun too.

De Lieve

MAP P.96, POCKET MAP B11
St-Margrietstraat 1 ☎ 09 223 29 47,
🌐 eetkaffee-delieve.be. Mon–Fri
11.30am–2.30pm & 6–10pm.

On the edge of the Patershol, this informal, bistro-style restaurant features traditional Flemish dishes that taste simply wonderful – don't miss the risotto with wild mushrooms or the rabbit with prunes. Main courses are very reasonable at around €20. A popular spot with so-called BVs – *Bekende Vlamingen* (Famous Flemings).

Maison Elza

MAP P.96, POCKET MAP B12
Jan Breydelstraat 36 ☎ 09 225 21
28, 🌐 maisonelza.be. Sat, Sun & Mon
9am–9.30pm.

Idiosyncratic, split-level café-restaurant that's liberally sprinkled

Holy Food

with Edwardian bric-a-brac – you'll even spot some vintage models' dummies. They serve a tasty breakfast here and afternoon teas and in the evening the dinner menu offers a limited but well-chosen selection of freshly prepared meat and fish dishes (mains average €25): try the wood pigeon risotto. The window tables overlook a canal and, if the weather holds, you can eat out on the pontoon at the back.

Marco Polo Trattoria

MAP P.96, POCKET MAP C12
Serpentstraat 11 ☎ 09 225 04 20. Tues–Sat
6–10pm.

This simple rustic restaurant is part of the Italian "slow food" movement in which the emphasis is on organic, seasonal ingredients prepared in a traditional manner. The menu is small, but all the dishes are freshly prepared and delicious. Mains from €20, pizzas €12.

Midtown Grill

MAP P.96, POCKET MAP B13
Korenlei 10 ☎ 09 269 77 44, 🌐 midtown
grill.be. Daily noon–2.30pm & 6–10pm.

It's surprisingly difficult to find a good-quality restaurant that's open

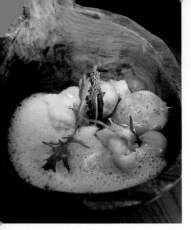

Naturell

on Sunday here in Ghent – so this smart medium-sized place can fill the gap. Attached to the *Marriott Hotel* (see page 134), meat dominates the menu – especially steak at around €35. There is a bit of tomfoolery with the specialist steak knives – but nothing too unbearable.

Naturell

MAP P.96, POCKET MAP B12
Jan Breydelstraat 10 ☎ 09 279 07 08,
Ⓦ naturell-gent.be. Tues 7–10.30pm, Wed–Sat noon–3pm & 7–10.30pm.
The brightly coloured furnishings and fittings may be informal, but they take their food very seriously here with the emphasis on local, seasonal ingredients used in high-octane, haute cuisine set meals. A five-course meal will set you back €75, a three-course lunch €35. Reservations are essential.

Du Progrès

MAP P.96, POCKET MAP C13
Korenmarkt 10 ☎ 09 225 17 16,
Ⓦ duprogres.be. Tues–Sat 11.30am–10pm.
This long-established, family-owned restaurant is popular with tourists and locals alike – and with good reason. The house speciality is steaks (€25–30) – and very tasty they are too. Rapid-fire service and a handy central location.

De Raadkamer

MAP P.96, POCKET MAP B15
Nederkouter 3 ☎ 09 233 68 49,
Ⓦ de-raadkamer.be. Tues–Sat noon–2.30pm & 6–9.30pm & Sun noon–2.30pm.
Family-run restaurant in neat, modern premises offering a short but well-conceived menu of Belgian favourites, such as the turbot risotto with asparagus and lobster sauce. Mains average €23. Impeccable service.

Roots

MAP P.96, POCKET MAP C12
Vrouwebroersstraat 5 ☎ 09 310 67 73,
Ⓦ rootsgent.be. Mon–Fri except Wed noon–1.30pm & 7–8.30pm; Wed 7–8.30pm.
This cool and collected Patershol haunt, hidden away behind its ancient brickwork, may have the simplest of boho decor, but the menu is subtle and complex and always features local, seasonal ingredients. Pumpkin and parmesan with red gurnard gives the flavour. Fixed menus are the order of the day here – €28 at lunch times, €55 at night.

Bars and clubs

't Dreupelkot

MAP P.96, POCKET MAP C12
Groentenmarkt 12 ☎ 09 224 21 20,
Ⓦ dreupelkot.be. Daily: July & Aug from 6pm until late; Sept–June from 4pm until late.
Cosy bar specializing in *jenever* (Dutch gin), of which it stocks more than 200 brands, all kept at icy temperatures – the vanilla flavour is particularly delicious. It's down a little alley leading off the Groentenmarkt – and next door to *Het Waterhuis* (see page 117).

Dulle Griet

MAP P.96, POCKET MAP C12
Vrijdagmarkt 50 ☎ 09 224 24 55,
Ⓦ dullegriet.be. Mon 4.30pm–1am, Tues–Sat noon–1am, Sun noon–7.30pm.
Long, dark and atmospheric bar with all manner of incidental bygones – with barrels and puppets

hanging from the ceiling and vintage vehicle number plates on the walls. But the magnet is the beer – over 500 different brews either on tap or bottled.

Hotsy Totsy

MAP P.96, POCKET MAP A13
Hoogstraat 1 🕿 09 224 20 12. Mon–Fri from 6pm till late, Sat & Sun from 8pm.
Long the gathering place of the city's intelligentsia – though less so today – this ornately decorated bar, with its Art Nouveau flourishes, has ranks of drinkers lining up along its long wooden bar. Regular live jazz and blues sessions too.

De Trollekelder

MAP P.96, POCKET MAP D12
Bij St-Jacobs 17 🕿 0477 40 92 37, Ⓦ trollekelder.be. Mon–Thurs 4pm–2am & Fri–Sun 3pm–2am.
This dark and atmospheric bar offers a huge selection of beers in an ancient merchant's house – don't be deterred by the trolls in the window.

Den Turk

MAP P.96, POCKET MAP C13
Botermarkt 3 🕿 09 233 01 97, Ⓦ cafeden turk.be. Daily from 11am until late.
Thought to be the oldest bar in the city, this tiny rabbit warren of a place offers a tasty range of beers and whiskies and attracts an older

clientele. The decor is mixed – some of the rooms are rather dull, others are high Victorian with plenty of varnished wood. Frequent live music, mainly jazz.

't Velootje

MAP P.96, POCKET MAP C11
Kalversteeg 2 🕿 09 223 28 34. Daily noon–2am.
Ghent has always had more than its fair share of quirky pubs and bars – and this cramped and crowded place, deep in the Patershol, is a real humdinger, its interior jam packed with a menagerie of ancient clutter, especially bikes. Has a good range of bottled beers, but to avoid a surprise, check the price before you buy.

Het Waterhuis aan de Bierkant

MAP P.96, POCKET MAP C12
Groentenmarkt 9 🕿 09 225 06 80, Ⓦ waterhuisaandebierkant.be. Daily 11am–1am.
More than a hundred types of beer are available in this engaging canal-side bar, which is popular with both tourists and older locals. Be sure to try Stropken (literally "noose"), a delicious local brew named after the time, in 1540, when Charles V compelled the rebellious city burghers to parade outside the town gate with ropes around their necks.

Dulle Griet

Southern and eastern Ghent

Although the majority of Ghent's leading attractions are within easy strolling distance of the Korenmarkt, three of the city's principal museums are located some 2km south of the centre. The nearest is STAM, an ingenious and well-conceived museum that tracks through the city's history from its premises on the sprawling campus of what was once the old Cistercian Bijlokeabdij (Bijloke Abbey). A little further afield are both MSK (Museum voor Schone Kunsten), with Ghent's most comprehensive collection of fine art, and the adjacent Museum of Contemporary Art, known as S.M.A.K. Many visitors just hop on a tram at the Korenmarkt for the quick trip down to the three, but with a little more time the twenty-minute walk there makes for a reasonably pleasant and very easy stroll. East of St-Baafskathedraal, Ghent's eighteenth- and nineteenth-century suburbs stretch out toward the Dampoort train station. Few tourists venture this way, which is a pity as this is a particularly interesting part of Ghent, though there is only one specific sight as such, the enchanting ruins of St-Baafsabdij (St Bavo's Abbey).

STAM

STAM

MAP P.122, POCKET MAP A16–B16
Bijlokesite, Godshuizenlaan ☎ 09 267 14
00, ⓦ stamgent.be. Mon–Fri except Wed
9am–5pm, Sat & Sun 10am–6pm. €8.
Once wealthy and powerful, the
former Cistercian **Bijlokeabdij**
(Bijloke Abbey), just to the west
of the River Leie, dates from the
thirteenth century. Much of the
medieval complex has survived
and, with subsequent additions,
now occupies a sprawling multi-
use site. At its core is **STAM**, an
ambitious museum which explores
the city's history via paintings
and a battery of original artefacts.
Visits begin in a bright, modern
cube-like structure and continue
in the former abbey church and
cloisters, with one of the early
highlights being the two delightful
medieval wall paintings in the
former refectory. Look out also
for the room full of medieval
illuminated books and incidental
sculpture; a selection of vintage
military hardware; a good section
on the city's guilds; and, the pick
of the lot, a detailed section on the
mysterious theft of **The Just Judges
panel** of the *Adoration of the Mystic
Lamb* (see page 110).

Citadelpark

MAP P.122, POCKET MAP B18
Koning Léopold II-laan. Open access; free.
A large chunk of greenery,
Citadelpark takes its name from
the fortress that stood here until
the 1870s, when the land was
cleared and prettified with the
addition of grottoes and ponds,
statues and fountains, a waterfall
and a bandstand. These nineteenth-
century niceties survive today and,
as an added bonus, a network of
footpaths crisscross the park. Even
better, if you have spent much
time in Ghent, which is almost
universally flat, Citadelpark seems
refreshingly hilly. In the 1940s, a
large brick complex was built on
the east side of the park and, after
various incarnations, it now divides

A statue in Citadelpark

into two – a Conference Centre
and the **S.M.A.K. art gallery**.

S.M.A.K. (Stedelijk Museum voor Actuele Kunst)

MAP P.122, POCKET MAP C18
Jan Hoetplein 1 ☎ 09 240 76 01, ⓦ smak.
be. Tues–Fri 9.30am–5.30pm, Sat & Sun
10am–6pm. €8.
S.M.A.K. (Municipal Museum
of Contemporary Art) is one of
Belgium's most adventurous and
experimental contemporary art
galleries. Nowadays, it's largely
devoted to temporary displays of
international standing and these
exhibitions are supplemented
by a regularly rotated selection
of sculptures, paintings and
installations drawn from the
museum's wide-ranging permanent
collection. S.M.A.K. possesses
examples of all the major artistic
movements since World War II
– everything from surrealism, the
CoBrA group and pop art through
to minimalism and conceptual
art, as well as their forerunners,
most notably René Magritte and
Paul Delvaux. Perennial favourites
include the installations of the
influential German **Joseph Beuys**

(1921–86), who played a leading role in the European avant-garde art movement of the 1970s; the Belgian **Panamarenko**'s (b.1940) eccentric polyester zeppelin entitled *Aeromodeller*, and a characteristically unnerving painting by Dublin-born **Francis Bacon** (1909–92) entitled *A Figure Sitting*.

MSK (Museum voor Schone Kunsten)

MAP P.122, POCKET MAP C18
Fernand Scribedreef 1 ☎ 09 323 67 00, ⓦ mskgent.be. Tues–Fri 9.30–5.30pm; Sat & Sun 10am–6pm. €8.

One of the city's prime attractions, **MSK** (Fine Art Museum), just opposite S.M.A.K., holds the city's principal art collection and runs an ambitious programme of temporary exhibitions. It occupies an imposing Neoclassical edifice and the paintings are well displayed, but the interior can be a tad confusing – be sure to pick up a floor plan at reception.

In Room 2, one highlight of the museum's small but eclectic collection of early Flemish paintings is **Rogier van der Weyden**'s (1399–1464) *Madonna with*

MSK

Carnation, a charming work where the proffered flower, in all its exquisite detail, serves as a symbol of Christ's passion. Also in Room 2 are two superb works by **Hieronymus Bosch** (1450–1516), his *Bearing of the Cross* showing Christ mocked by some of the most grotesque and deformed characters he ever painted. Among the grotesques, you'll spy a singularly wan penitent thief confessing to a monstrously ugly monk and St Veronica, whose cloak carries the imprint of Christ's face. This struggle between good and evil is also the subject of Bosch's *St Jerome at Prayer*, in the foreground of which the saint prays, surrounded by a brooding, menacing landscape.

Room 5 features a powerful *St Francis* by **Rubens** (1577–1640), in which a very sick-looking saint bears the marks of the stigmata, and **Jacob Jordaens** (1593–1678), who was greatly influenced by Rubens, is well represented in Room 7 by the whimsical romanticism of his *Allegory of Fertility*. Jordaens was, however, capable of much greater subtlety and his *Studies of the Head of Abraham Grapheus*, also in Room 7, is an example of the high-quality preparatory paintings he completed, most of which were later recycled within larger compositions. In the same room, **Anthony van Dyck**'s (1599–1641) *Jupiter and Antiope* wins the bad taste award for its portrayal of the lecherous god with his tongue hanging out in anticipation of sex with a sleeping Antiope. Further on, Room 15 holds a fine collection of seventeenth-century Dutch genre paintings plus several works by Kortrijk's talented **Roelandt Savery** (1576–1639), who trained in Amsterdam and worked for the Habsburgs in Prague and Vienna before returning to the Low Countries. To suit the tastes of his German patrons, he infused many of his landscapes with the romantic classicism that they preferred – Orpheus and the Garden of Eden

Vooruit performing arts centre

wcrc two favourite subjects – but the finely observed detail of his paintings was always in the true Flemish tradition as in his striking *Plundering of a Village*, where there's a palpable sense of outrage.

The museum's eighteenth- and nineteenth-century collection includes a handful of romantic historical canvases, plus – and this is a real surprise – a superbly executed portrait of a certain *Alexander Edgar* by the Scot **Henry Raeburn** (1756–1823). Also on display are several key paintings by Ostend's **James Ensor** (1860–1949), notably the ghoulish *Skeleton looking at Chinoiserie and Pierrot and Skeleton in Yellow Robe*, though you have to take pot luck with the museum's most famous Ensor, his much-lauded *Self-Portrait with Flower Hat*, as this is often out on loan. Other high points include a batch of Expressionist paintings by the likes of **Constant Permeke** (1886–1952) and **Gustave de Smet** (1887–1943) as well as several characteristically unsettling works by both **Paul Delvaux** (1897–1994) and **René Magritte** (1898–1967). Two cases in point are Delvaux's *The Staircase* and Magritte's *Perspective II*, Manet's *Balcony*, in which wooden coffins have replaced the figures from Manet's painting.

Vooruit

MAP P.122, POCKET MAP D15
St-Pietersnieuwstraat 23 ☏ 09 267 28 48, Ⓦ vooruit.be. Café-bar: Sun–Wed noon–1am; Thurs–Sat noon–2am.
The **Vooruit** performing arts centre (see page 147) has good claim to be the cultural centre of the city (at least for the under-40s), offering a wide-ranging programme of rock and pop through to dance. It also occupies a splendid building, a twin-towered and turreted former festival hall that was built for Ghent's socialists in an eclectic rendition of Art Nouveau in 1914.

Overpoortstraat

MAP P.122, POCKET MAP C17–C18
Running south from Vooruit, **St-Pietersnieuwstraat** and then **Overpoortstraat** cut through the heart of the city's student quarter, a gritty and grimy but vivacious district, jam-packed with late-night bars and cafés. En route is one of Ghent's biggest churches, **St-Pietersabdij** (St Peter's Abbey; see page below).

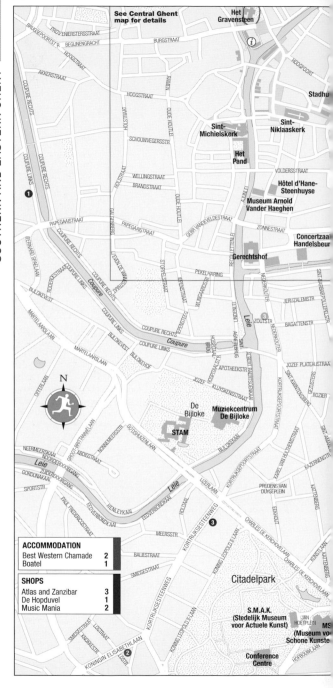

See Central Ghent map for details

Het Gravensteen

BRUGSEPOORTSTRAAT R
PROVENIERSSTERSSTRAAT
BEGIJNENGRACHT
HOOGSTRAAT
BURGSTRAAT

AKKERSTRAAT

COUPURE RECHTS

COUPURE LINKS

HOOGSTRAAT

Stadhu

RAMEN

OUDE HOUTLEI

HOLSTRAAT

SCHOUWVEGERSSTR

Sint-Michielskerk

Sint-Niklaaskerk

VOLDERSSTRAAT

Het Pand

WELLINGSTRAAT

BRANDSTRAAT

Hôtel d'Hane-Steenhuyse

GALGENBERG

HOLSTRAAT

OUDE HOUTLEI

AJUINLEI

Museum Arnold Vander Haeghen

PAPEGAAISTRAAT

COUPURE RECHTS

PAPEGAAISTRAAT

LEDEN DE VRIESESTRAAT

GEBR VAN DE VELDESTRAAT

ZONNESTRAAT

Concertzaal Handelsbeur

BERNARD SPAELAAN

DODECESTRAAT

COUPURE LINKS

COUPURE RECHTS

STOPFELSTRAAT

Gerechtshof

RECATTENLEI

PEKELHARING

NEERKOUTER

SINT-BARBARAPOLLEPELSTR

BULOKEVEST

COUPURE RECHTS

COUPURE LINKS

BULOKEVEST

WIJNGAARDSTR

IEPERSTRAAT

KEERSSTEEG

JERUZALEMSTR

BAGATTENSTR

MARTELAARSLAAN

BULOKEVEST

COUPURE LINKS

COUPURE RECHTS

COUPURE LINKS

Coupure

BULOKHOF

Lele

ZOLTSTR

NEERKOUTER

JOZEF PLATEAUSTRAA

DEELELAAN

N

MARTELAARSLAAN

JOZEF

KLUYSKENSSTRAAT

SINT-AGNETENBRUG

SINT-KWINTENSBERG

ROZIER

NEERMEERSKAAI

NOORDERDOOGANG

GORDUNAKAAI

SPORTSTR

GROT-BRITTANIELAAN

GOT BABTINE LAAN

NONENMEERSTR

GOTSHUIZENLAAN

ABDISSTRAAT

De Bijloke

Muziekcentrum De Bijloke

STAM

BIJLOKEKAAI

APOTHEEKSTR

KORTRIJKSEPOORTSTRAAT

BELLEVUEHOF TERP

KAZERNENSTR

SINT-MAANS

HEMELRYKAAN

EEDVERBONDKAAI

HOLDAAL

IJZERLAAN

KORTRIJKSEPOORTSTRAAT

PRUDENS VAN DUYSEPLEIN

EEKHOUT

KATTEBERG

MEERSSTR

BALIESTRAAT

SMIDSESTRAAT

KORTRIJKSESTEENWEG

KONING LEOPOLD II LAAN

CHARLES DE KERCHOVELAAN

CHARLES DE KERCHOVELAAN

Citadelpark

KONINGIN ELISABETHLAAN

LIJSTR

KONING LEOPOLD II LAAN

S.M.A.K. (Stedelijk Museum voor Actuele Kunst)

JAN HOETPLEIN

MS (Museum vo Schone Kunste

Conference Centre

HOFBOUWLAAN

ACCOMMODATION	
Best Western Chamade	2
Boatel	1

SHOPS	
Atlas and Zanzibar	3
De Hopduvel	1
Music Mania	2

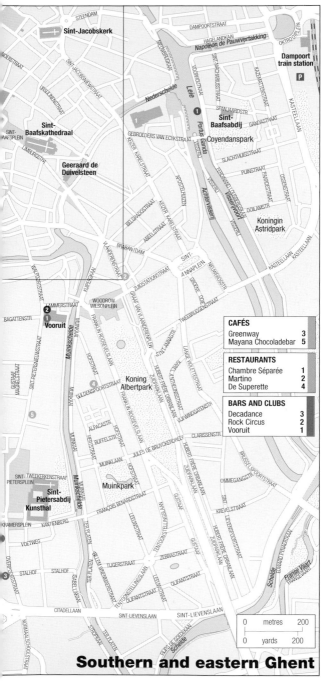

STEENDAM

Sint-Jacobskerk

DAMPOORTSTRAAT

Napoleon de Pauwvertakking
HAGELANDKAAI

Dampoort
train station

Nederschelde

Sint-
Baafsabdij

Sint-Baafskathedraal

Coyendanspark

GEBROEDERS VAN EYCKSTRAAT

Geeraard de
Duivelsteen

SLACHTHUISSTRAAT

Koningin
Astridpark

SINT-
ANNAPLEIN

WOODROW
WILSONPLEIN

Vooruit

Koning
Albertpark

CAFÉS
| Greenway | 3 |
| Mayana Chocoladebar | 5 |

RESTAURANTS
Chambre Séparée	1
Martino	2
De Superette	4

BARS AND CLUBS
Decadance	3
Rock Circus	2
Vooruit	1

Muinkpark

Sint-
Pietersabdij
Kunsthal

CITADELLAAN

SINT-LIEVENSLAAN

| 0 | metres | 200 |
| 0 | yards | 200 |

Southern and eastern Ghent

St-Pietersabdij

St-Pietersabdij

MAP P.122, POCKET MAP D17
St-Pietersplein ☏ 09 210 10 75,
🅦 sintpietersabdij.stad.gent. Church,
gardens & most of the complex: Tues–Sun
10am–6pm. Free. Kunsthal: same hours,
but admission sometimes charged; Alison:
same hours, but €4.

The sprawling mass of **St-
Pietersabdij** (St Peter's Abbey)
flanks St-Pietersplein, a very wide
and very long cobbled square. The
abbey dates back to the earliest
days of the city and was probably
founded by St Amand in about
640. The Vikings razed the original
buildings three centuries later, but
it was rebuilt on a grand scale and
became rich and powerful in equal
measure. In 1578, the Protestants
destroyed the abbey as a symbol
of much that they hated and the
present complex – a Baroque
whopper incorporating a church
and two courtyard complexes –
was erected in the seventeenth
and eighteenth centuries. The last
monks were ejected during the
French occupation of the 1790s and
since then – as with many other
ecclesiastical complexes in Belgium
– it's been hard to figure out any

suitable use. Today, much of the
complex serves as municipal offices,
but several sections are open to the
public, beginning with the domed
St-Pieterskerk, which was modelled
on St Peter's in Rome, though the
interior is no more than a plodding
Baroque. Elsewhere, there is a
small arts exhibition centre, the
Kunsthal St Pietersabdij, where
they feature temporary displays of
modern art and local history, and
you can wander the **gardens** with
their incidental ruins, herb garden,
orchard and mini-vineyard. Finally,
several of the abbey's cellars, rooms
and corridors can also be explored
with "**Alison**", a multilingual
audioguide geared up for teens and
pre-teens. There's precious little to
actually see here, but youngsters
seem to enjoy this miniature
labyrinth.

St-Baafsabdij

MAP P.122, POCKET MAP F13
Spanjaardstraat ☏ 09 210 10 75,
🅦 sintbaafsabdij.stad.gent. April–Oct Fri–
Sun 2–6pm. Free.

The extensive ruins of **St-
Baafsabdij** (St Bavo's Abbey)
ramble over a narrow parcel of land

The life and times of St Bavo

The patron saint of Ghent, **St Bavo** – or Baaf – was an early seventh century Frankish nobleman, who – in the way of such things – started out bad and then turned good. Fond of the drink and even fonder of his sword, Bavo led a wild and violent life until he was converted to Christianity by the French missionary St Amand. Thereafter, he gave his possessions to the poor and became a hermit-monk living in a hollow tree on the edge of Ghent. His remains were allegedly buried at St-Baafsabdij.

beside the River Leie, occupying what was once a strategically important location. It was here, in 630, that the French missionary St Amand (584–675) founded an abbey, though the locals could not have been overly impressed as they ended up drowning him in the river. Nonetheless, St Amand's abbey flourished as a place of pilgrimage on account of its guardianship of the remains of St Bavo (622–659). In the ninth century, the abbey suffered a major disaster when the Vikings decided this was the ideal spot to camp while they raided the surrounding region, but order was eventually restored, another colony of monks moved in and the abbey was rebuilt in 950. The Emperor Charles V had most of this second abbey knocked down in the 1540s and the monks decamped to St Baafskathedraal, but somehow the ruins managed to survive. Tucked away behind a stone retaining wall, the abbey's extensive **ruins** include the remnants of an ivy-covered Gothic cloister, whose long, vaulted corridors are attached to a distinctive, octagonal tower, comprising a toilet on the bottom floor and the storage room – the *sanctuarium* – for the St Bavo relic up above. Attached to the cloister is a substantial two-storey building, whose lower level holds all sorts of architectural bits and pieces retrieved from the city during renovations and demolitions. There are gargoyles and finely carved Gothic heads, terracotta panels,

broken off chunks of columns and capitals, and several delightful mini-tableaux. There's precious little labelling, but it's the skill of the carving that impresses and, if you've already explored the city, one or two pieces are identifiable, principally the original lion from the old punishment post on St-Veerleplein (see page 103).

Close by, a flight of steps leads up to the Romanesque **refectory**, a splendid chamber whose magnificent, hooped timber roof dates – remarkably enough – from the twelfth century. The grounds of the abbey are small, but they are partly wild, a flurry of shrubs and flowers that are absolutely delightful – and perfect for a picnic.

St-Baafsabdij

Shops

Atlas and Zanzibar

MAP P.122; POCKET MAP B17
Kortrijksesteenweg 19 ⓘ 09 220 87 99,
ⓦ atlaszanzibar.be. Mon–Sat 10am–1pm
& 2–6.pm.

Outstanding travel bookshop with
a comprehensive range of English-
language travel guide books, road
and hiking maps. They also sell
globes, extreme sports guides and
educational toys. Well-informed
staff will help you on your way.
About 2km south of the city centre.

De Hopduvel

MAP P.122, POCKET MAP A14
Coupure Links 625 ⓘ 09 225 20 68.
ⓦ dehopduvel.be. Tues–Sat 10am–6pm.

Named after a mischievous folklore
figure, the "Hop Devil", this
capacious store, in premises that
started out as an engine factory,
sells a comprehensive range of
Belgian beers at competitive prices.
Also has major sidelines in wines,
liquors, sparkling wines and home-
brew kits.

Mayana Chocoladebar

Music Mania

MAP P.122, POCKET MAP D15
St-Pietersnieuwstraat 19 ⓘ 09 278 23
38, ⓦ musicmaniarecords.be. Mon–Sat
11am–6.30pm.

Opened way back in the late 1960s,
this excellent record shop sells vinyl
in just about every musical genre
you can think of – from jazz, blues
and folk through to disco and
Afro-funk. It's mostly second-hand
stuff, but there are reissues and new
vinyl too. If you are familiar with
Ghent's live-music scene, you may
spy some big-name DJs.

Cafés

Greenway

MAP P.122, POCKET MAP C15
Nederkouter 42. ⓘ 09 269 07 69,
ⓦ greenway.be. Mon–Sat 11am–10pm.

Straightforward café-cum-takeaway
decorated in sharp modern style,
selling a wide range of eco-friendly
foods, from bio-burgers to pastas,
noodles and baguettes, all for just a
few euros.

Mayana Chocoladebar

MAP P.122, POCKET MAP D16
St-Pietersnieuwstraat 99. ⓘ 0497 40 34
04, ⓦ mayana.be. Mon–Thurs 1–11pm,
Fri–Sat 1–6pm, closed Sun.

Chocolate aficionados will get their
fix in this bright and modern café
devoted to the cocoa bean. Treats
on offer range from the humble
chocolate chip cookie to a chocolate
fondue for two, as well as a plethora
of chocolate-flavoured drinks – and
coffee. Takeaway available.

Restaurants

Chambre Séparée

MAP P.122, POCKET MAP E13
Keizer Karelstraat 1. ⓦ chambreseparee.
be. No phone; website bookings only.
Advance reservations essential; book well
in advance. Wed–Sat 6.30pm–11.30pm.

Prestige restaurant showcasing
the skills of one of Belgium's best-

known chefs – Kobe Desramaults. The decor is part of the charm of the place, eschewing the smart and formal for all things boho and distressed with the kitchen in full view. Located on the ground-floor of a brutalist former office block, which is often deemed to be Ghent's ugliest building – a Desramaults irony. Tasting menu only at an eye-watering €230.

Martino

MAP P.122, POCKET MAP E15
Vlaanderenstraat 125. ☏ 09 225 01 04. Daily except Wed & Thurs 11.30am–midnight.

Something of a local institution, this unpretentious, family-owned place is a diner-like affair with a workers' menu – steaks, burgers, sandwiches and a local favourite, the Martino, comprising raw beef with mustard, Tabasco, tomato and anchovy. A tasty spaghetti Bolognese costs just €13, crevettes €23.

De Superette

MAP P.122, POCKET MAP D16
Guldenspoorstraat 29. ⓦ de-superette.be. No phone; website bookings only. Wed–Fri 6–10pm, Sat & Sun 10am–4pm & 6–10pm.

In former industrial premises, this relaxed and informal café-restaurant is another (and more affordable) venture of top-draw chef Kobe Desramaults (see above). Fixed-menu brunches (€35) include pastries, cold meats, an egg dish and so forth, whilst dinners, which always include their delicious pizza, cost €38. Takeaway too.

Bars and clubs

Decadance

MAP P.122, POCKET MAP C18
Overpoortstraat 76 ☏ 09 329 00 54, ⓦ decadence.be. Times vary, see website, but core hours Fri & Sat 11pm–10am.

Long a standard-bearer for the city's nightlife, this club near the university (hence the abundance of students) offers one of the city's

De Superette

best nights out, with either live music – most of Belgium's bands have played here at one time or another – or DJs. Three rooms with three styles of music: reggae, hip-hop, drum 'n' bass and garage-techno vibes etc.

Rock Circus

MAP P.122, POCKET MAP C17
Overpoortstraat 22. ⓦ rockcircus. moonfruit.com. Mon–Sat 3pm–3am.

At the heart of the student quarter, this busy sometimes raucous bar prides itself on its range of beers – 58 or so on draft and a further regiment of bottled beers.

Vooruit

MAP P.122, POCKET MAP D15
St-Pietersnieuwstraat 23 ☏ 09 267 28 48, ⓦ vooruit.be. Café-bar: Sun–Wed noon–1am, Thurs–Sat noon–2am.

The Vooruit performing arts centre (see page 147) offers a wide range of rock, pop and jazz concerts plus dance and DJ nights. The main area, the ground-floor café-bar, is short of creature comforts – it's a large barn-like affair – but it attracts an avant-garde crew and gets jam-packed on the weekend.

ACCOMMODATION

De Orangerie, Bruges

Accommodation

The great thing about staying in either Bruges or Ghent is that most of the more enjoyable hotels and B&Bs are in or near the centre, which is exactly where you want to be. The main difference is that in Bruges you're spoilt for choice as the city has literally scores of places, whereas Ghent has a more limited – albeit just as select – range. An added bonus is that almost everywhere you'll be offered breakfast at no extra (or minimal) charge, ranging from a roll and coffee at the less expensive places through to full-scale banquets at the top end of the range. In Bruges, less so in Ghent, you'll also find that most of the hotels are small – twenty rooms, often fewer – and chains are few and far between. In both cities, standards are generally high among the hotels and B&Bs, a tad more inconsistent when you come to the hostels. One word of caution, however, is that many hotels offer rooms of widely divergent size and comfort – be pushy if you have to be – and some hoteliers are wont to deck out their foyers rather grandly, in contrast to the spartan rooms beyond.

Bruges

Bruges has over a hundred hotels, almost two hundred B&Bs and several youth hostels, but still can't accommodate all its visitors at busy times, especially in the high season (roughly late June to early Sept) and at Christmas – so you'd be well advised to **book ahead**. Most of the city's hotels are small – twenty rooms, often fewer – and few are chains. Standards are generally high among the hotels and B&Bs, whereas the city's hostels are more inconsistent. We've reviewed a batch of the best places below and there are comprehensive listings on the city's official tourist website (ⓦ visitbruges.be).

Hotels in Bruges

ADORNES MAP P.72, POCKET MAP D4. St Annarei 26 ⓣ 050 34 13 36, ⓦ adornes. be. Doubles from €135. Medium-sized three-star hotel in two tastefully converted old Flemish town house, with a plain, high-gabled facade. Both the public areas and the comfortable bedrooms are decorated in bright whites and creams, which emphasizes the antique charm of the place. It's in an excellent location, too, at the junction of two canals near the east end of Spiegelre. It's very child-friendly, with high chairs in the dining room so children can enjoy the delicious breakfast too.

ALEGRIA MAP P.72, POCKET MAP C5. St-Jakobsstraat 34 ⓣ 050 33 09 37, ⓦ alegria-hotel.com. Doubles from €120. Formerly a B&B, this appealing, family-run three-star hotel has a dozen or so large and attractive rooms in a central location, near the Markt. The rooms at the back, overlooking the garden, are quieter than those at the front. The owner is a mine of information about where and what to eat.

ARAGON MAP P.72, POCKET MAP C5. Naaldenstraat 22 ⓣ 050 33 35 33, ⓦ aragon.be/en. Doubles from €120. Behind its attractive, elongated facade, this four-star hotel has a wide range of rooms –

Hotel stars and prices

All licensed **Belgian hotels** carry a blue permit shield indicating the number of **stars** allocated (up to a maximum of five). This classification system is, by necessity, measured against easily identifiable criteria – toilets, room service, lifts, and so on – rather than aesthetics or specific location, and consequently can only provide a general guide as to quality and prices. In our listings in this chapter we have provided a **headline price** at the end of each and every hotel review. This indicates the **lowest price** you are likely to pay for a double or twin room during busy periods, though prices do fluctuate wildly depending on demand. At hostels, there is much less price fluctuation and we have provided the cost of both a dormitory bed and a double room.

from budget to executive – located in both the main building and the neighbouring annexe. The decor is crisp and modern, the hotel friendly and well-run. The location is convenient too – beside a narrow but particularly attractive side street, a five-minute walk from the Markt.

CORDOEANIER MAP P.38, POCKET MAP C5. Cordoeaniersstraat 18 ☎ 050 33 90 51, ⓦ cordoeanier.be. Doubles from €95. Medium-sized, family-run two-star hotel handily located in a narrow side street a couple of minutes' walk north of the Burg. Mosquitoes can be a problem here, but the 22 rooms are neat, trim and modern.

EUROP MAP P.72, POCKET MAP C4. Augustijnenrei 18 ☎ 050 33 79 75, ⓦ hoteleurop.com. Doubles from €95. Three-star hotel in a late-nineteenth-century town house overlooking a canal about five minutes' walk north of the Burg. The public areas are somewhat frumpy and the modern bedrooms distinctly spartan, but the prices are very competitive.

FEVERY MAP P.72, POCKET MAP D3. Collaert Mansionsstraat 3 ☎ 050 33 12 69, ⓦ hotelfevery.be/en. Doubles from €69. With good eco credentials – saving water, waste and energy – this unassuming, three-star hotel occupies a substantial, albeit standard-issue, three-storey brick building on a pleasant side street about 15 minutes' walk north of the Burg. The rooms are neat, trim, modern and competitively priced: the smallest doubles cost €69 – with a bit more space for an extra €10.

DE GOEZEPUT MAP P.48, POCKET MAP B7. Goezeputstraat 29 ☎ 050 34 26 94, ⓦ hotelgoezeput.be. Doubles from €95. In a charming location near the cathedral, this enjoyable two-star hotel occupies a thoroughly refurbished eighteenth-century convent. The guest rooms, which vary considerably in size, have been done out in contemporary style in shades of brown and cream, though the entrance, with its handsome wooden beams and staircase, has been left untouched.

JACOBS MAP P.72, POCKET MAP C4. Baliestraat 1 ☎ 050 33 98 31, ⓦ hotel jacobs.be. Doubles from €95. Pleasant three-star hotel set in a creatively modernized old-brick building complete with a precipitous crow-step gable. The twenty-odd rooms are decorated in brisk modern style, though some are a little small. It's in a quiet location in an attractive part of the centre, a ten-minute walk northeast of the Markt.

JAN BRITO MAP P.38, POCKET MAP D6. Freren Fonteinstraat 1 ☎ 050 33 06 01, ⓦ janbrito.com/en. Doubles from €130. Something of a mixed bag of a place, the best (and most expensive) guest rooms at this large and rambling hotel are in the restored patrician mansion at the front. Most of the rooms are, however, in the more modest brick annexe at the back – and they are ok if nothing special; the same applies to the breakfasts. Handily located, a short walk from the Burg.

MONSIEUR ERNEST MAP P.48, POCKET MAP B6. Wulfhagestraat 43 ☎ 050 96 09 66,

Top picks

Luxury:
Bruges: De Orangerie (see page 132); Ghent: Sandton Grand Hotel (see page 135).

Charming:
Bruges: Ter Duinen (see page 132); Ghent: Erasmus (see page 134).

Family:
Bruges: Adornes (see page 130); Ghent: Harmony (see page 134).

Location:
Bruges: Die Swaene (see page 132); Ghent: Boatel (see page 134).

Budget:
Bruges: Jacobs (see page 131); Ghent: Monasterium Poortackere (see page 131).

Ⓦ monsieurernest.com. Doubles from €125. Sister to the Monsieur Maurice (see below), this agreeable, smallish hotel with its unassuming brick facade occupies tastefully modernized premises with neat and trim modern rooms, and a splendid staircase as a reminder of grander times. It's located beside a canal on an appealing side street to the west of the Markt, although this is only visible from a couple of rooms. Minimum two-night stay.

MONSIEUR MAURICE MAP P.72, POCKET MAP B5. Leeuwstraat 8 ☏ 050 61 63 60, Ⓦ monsieurmaurice.eu. Doubles from €125. Despite its somewhat utilitarian exterior, this very agreeable three-star hotel has a well-maintained, modern interior with vinyl floors. It's in an attractive location, next to a canal in a quiet part of the centre, but only one or two of the rooms views of the water.

MONTANUS MAP P.48, POCKET MAP D7. Nieuwe Gentweg 76 ☏ 050 33 11 76, Ⓦ denheerd.be. Doubles from €120. This four-star hotel occupies a big old house that has been sympathetically modernized with simple yet luxurious decor. The twelve rooms are large, comfortable and modern – and there are twelve more at the back, in chalet-like accommodation at the far end of the large garden. The garden also accommodates an up-market restaurant.

NAVARRA MAP P.72, POCKET MAP B5. St-Jakobsstraat 41 ☏ 050 34 05 61, Ⓦ hotelnavarra.com. Doubles from €170. This immaculate four-star hotel occupies one of the city's finest buildings, a

handsome mansion built in the French style in the early eighteenth-century. The grand facade, with its balanced symmetries, has an elegant open courtyard at the front and a garden terrace at the back. There are nigh-on 100 guest rooms here and although they don't quite match the setting – most are modern – they are still very comfortable. On a busy street, just north of the Markt.

DE ORANGERIE MAP P.38, POCKET MAP C6. Kartuizerinnenstraat 10 ☏ 050 34 16 49, Ⓦ hotelorangerie.be. Doubles from €200. In a former convent and one-time bakery, this classy, family-owned, four-star hotel has twenty guest rooms, the pick of which are kitted out in an exuberant version of country-house style. The wood-panelled lounge oozes a relaxed and demure charm – as does the breakfast room – and a tunnel leads down to a canalside terrace. It's a great central location, too.

DIE SWAENE MAP P.38, POCKET MAP D6. Steenhouwersdijk 1 ☏ 050 34 27 98, Ⓦ dieswaene.com. Doubles from €130. In a perfect location, beside a particularly pretty and peaceful section of canal close to the Burg, this long-established, four-star hotel has thirty guest rooms decorated in an individual and rather sumptuous antique style. There's also a heated pool and sauna, and the breakfast will set you up for the best part of a day.

TER DUINEN MAP P.72, POCKET MAP D3. Langerei 52 ☏ 050 33 04 37, Ⓦ hotelterduinen.eu. Doubles from €140. Especially charming three-star hotel in a lovely part of the city, beside the Langerei canal, a fifteen-minute walk from the Markt. Occupying a beautifully maintained eighteenth-century villa, with period public areas and appealing modern rooms. Superb breakfasts, too.

B&Bs in Bruges

CÔTÉ CANAL MAP P.38, POCKET MAP D5. Hertsbergestraat 8–10 T0475 45 77 07, Ⓦ bruges-bedandbreakfast.be. Doubles from €17. Deluxe affair in a pair of handsome – and handsomely restored – eighteenth-century houses, with four large guest rooms/suites kitted out in grand period style down to the huge, flowing drapes. In a central location, with a garden that backs onto a canal.

HET WIT BEERTJE MAP P.48, POCKET MAP A7. Witte Beerstraat 4 Ⓣ 050 45 08 88, Ⓦ hetwitbeertje.be. Doubles from €85. This modest little guesthouse-cum-B&B, with just three en-suite rooms, is a particularly good deal. It's located about twenty-minute walk west of the Markt, beyond the Smedenpoort.

HUIS KONING MAP P.72, POCKET MAP B5. Oude Zak 25 Ⓣ 0476 25 08 12, Ⓦ huiskoning.be. Doubles from €120. A plushly renovated B&B in a seventeenth-century, step-gable terrace house with a pleasant canalside garden. The four en-suite guest rooms are decorated in a fresh, modern style and two have canal views.

NUMBER 11 MAP P.38, POCKET MAP D5. Peerdenstraat 11 Ⓣ 050 33 06 75, Ⓦ number11.be. Doubles from €150. In the heart of old Bruges, on a traffic-free side street, this first-rate B&B set in an ancient terrace house has just four lavish guest rooms – all wooden floors, beamed ceilings and expensive wallpaper. Every comfort is laid on, and the breakfasts are smashing.

SINT-NIKLAAS B&B MAP P.48, POCKET MAP C6. St-Niklaasstraat 18 Ⓣ 050 61 03 08, Ⓦ sintnik.be. Doubles from €145. In a good-looking, three-storey, eighteenth-century townhouse on a side street near the Markt, this well-kept B&B has three modern, en-suite guest rooms. One has a lovely view of the Belfort.

Hostels in Bruges

BRUGES EUROPA MAP P.48, POCKET MAP D9. Baron Ruzettelaan 143 Ⓣ 050 35 26 79, Ⓦ jeugdherbergen.be. Dorm beds from €24, doubles from €52. This is a good-value HI hostel set in its own grounds, but the large, institutional building is 2km south of the centre in the suburb of Assebroek. There are more than 200 beds in a mix of rooms from doubles through to twelve-bed dorms, most en suite. Breakfast is included in the price and there are security lockers, wi-fi, free parking, a bar and a lounge. City bus #2 from outside Bruges train station passes within 200m – ask the driver to let you off at the Wantestraat bus stop.

SNUFFEL HOSTEL MAP P.72, POCKET MAP B4. Ezelstraat 42 Ⓣ 050 33 31 33, Ⓦ hostel world.com. Dorms from €21.With its bright and cheery modernist facade, this is the best-looking hostel in Bruges by a country mile. With 120 beds and good facilities, including a fully equipped guest kitchen, showers, bicycle store, laundry and a patio/terrace.

ST CHRISTOPHER'S BAUHAUS MAP P.72, POCKET MAP F4. Langestraat 133–137 Ⓣ 050 34 10 93, Ⓦ bauhaus.be. Dorm beds from €20, doubles from €77. This lively, laid-back hostel, a 15min walk east of the Burg, has a boho air and offers a mishmash of rooms accommodating between two and sixteen bunks each, some with pod beds. Bike rental, lockers, a bar and café also available.

Ghent

Ghent has around sixty hotels, ranging from the delightful to the mundanely modern, with several of the most stylish and enjoyable – but not necessarily most expensive – located right in the centre.

There's also a small army of B&Bs, though these are more widely dispersed, and a couple of bright and cheerful hostels. The tourist information's website has comprehensive listings (Ⓦ visit.gent.be).

Hotels in Ghent

BEST WESTERN CHAMADE MAP P.122, POCKET MAP A19. Koningin Elisabethlaan 3 ☎ 09 220 15 15, ⓦ chamade.be. **Doubles from €140.** Standard, three-star accommodation in bright, modern bedrooms at this family-run hotel, which occupies a distinctive, six-storey modern block, a five-minute walk north of the train station.

BOATEL MAP P.122, POCKET MAP E13. Voorhuitkaai 44 ☎ 09 267 10 30, ⓦ the boatel.com. **Doubles from €125.** Arguably the most distinctive of the city's hotels, the two-star Boatel is, as its name implies, a converted boat – an imaginatively and immaculately refurbished canal barge to be precise. It's moored in one of the city's outer canals, a ten-to-fifteen-minute walk east from the centre. The seven bedrooms are decked out in crisp modern style, and breakfasts, taken on the poop deck, are very good.

ERASMUS MAP P.96, POCKET MAP B13. Poel 25 ☎ 09 224 21 95, ⓦ erasmushotel. be. **Doubles from €100.** Friendly, family-run two-star located in a commodious old town house a few metres away from the Korenlei. Each room is thoughtfully decorated and furnished in traditional style with lots of antiques. The breakfast is excellent and reservations are strongly advised in summer.

DE FLANDRE MAP P.96, POCKET MAP B13. Poel 1 ☎ 09 266 06 00, ⓦ hoteldeflandre. be. **Doubles from €110.** Medium-sized, four-star hotel in a thoroughly refashioned, nineteenth-century mansion with a modern annexe at the back. The rooms vary considerably in both size, style and comfort, and those towards the rear are much quieter than those on the road. Competitively priced.

GHENT MARRIOTT HOTEL MAP P.96, POCKET MAP B13. Korenlei 10 ☎ 09 233 93 93, ⓦ marriott.com. **Doubles from €250.** This smart and slick hotel may be part of an international chain, but full marks to the architects – both for the discrete pedestrian entry from the historic Korenlei to the capacious, arching glass ceiling enclosing reception, lounge and coffee bar. The rooms are banked up to the sides of the glass ceiling, but each is modern and comfortable.

The hotel restaurant – the Midtown Grill (see page 115) – is one of the very few restaurants in Ghent that is open on Sunday. Wide fluctuations in the price.

GHENT RIVER MAP P.96, POCKET MAP C12. Waaistraat 5 ☎ 09 266 10 10, ⓦ ghent-river-hotel.be. **Doubles from €120.** Four-star hotel whose austere modern facade doesn't do it any favours, but persevere: the interior is much more appealing and most of the guest rooms occupy that part of the building which was once a cotton mill – hence the bare-brick walls and industrial trappings.

HARMONY MAP P.96, POCKET MAP C12. Kraanlei 37 ☎ 09 324 26 80, ⓦ hotel-harmony.be. **Doubles from €170.** In an immaculately renovated old mansion, this deluxe four-star hotel has just twenty-odd guest rooms decorated in an attractive modern style – all wooden floors and shades of brown and cream. The best rooms are on the top floor and come complete with their own mini-terrace, affording grand views over the city.

MONASTERIUM POORTACKERE MAP P.96, POCKET MAP B13. Oude Houtlei 56 ☎ 09 269 22 10, ⓦ monasterium.be. **Doubles from €110.** This unusual one-star hotel-cum-guesthouse occupies a rambling and somewhat spartan former nunnery and orphanage, whose ageing brickwork dates from the nineteenth century. There's a choice of rooms, all en-suite, with the cheapest being doubles in the former doctor's house (€110); there are others in the old orphanage (€140; max 5 guests) and yet more offering a slightly more authentic experience in the former nuns' quarters (either 6 beds for €180 or doubles for €155). Breakfast is taken in the former chapterhouse. A five-minute walk west of Veldstraat.

NH GENT BELFORT MAP P.96, POCKET MAP C13. Hoogpoort 63 ☎ 09 233 33 31, ⓦ nh-hotels.com. **Doubles from €140.** Under previous owners, this chain hotel was one of the smartest in Ghent. Some of the gloss may have worn off, but it still has a great location – just across from the Stadhuis – and the 174 rooms are comfortable enough in a chain sort of way. There are three categories to choose from - standard, superior and executive – and a gym with sauna, too.

NOVOTEL CENTRUM MAP P.96, POCKET MAP C13. Goudenleeuwplein 5 ☎ 09 293 90 02, ⓦ novotel.com. Doubles from €90. The guest rooms at this brisk, three-star chain hotel are pretty routine, but the location near the Cathedral is hard to beat. The price is very competitive and there's an outdoor swimming pool – a rarity in central Ghent – which is great if the sun is out.

SANDTON GRAND HOTEL MAP P.96, POCKET MAP A13. Reylof Hoogstraat 36 ☎ 09 235 40 70, ⓦ sandton.eu. Doubles from €140. This superb chain hotel occupies a spacious nineteenth-century mansion, whose elegant, high-ceilinged foyer sets a perfect tone. Beyond, the 158 rooms vary in size and facilities, but most are immaculate, spacious and decorated in an appealing rendition of country-house style. The former coach house is now a spa and there is a patio terrace too. The least expensive deals exclude breakfast.

B&Bs in Ghent

ABRAHAMS PRINSENHOF MAP P.96, POCKET MAP B12. Abrahamstraat 5 ☎ 09 223 41 08, ⓦ dolders.be. Two guests in a suite per night €100. In an immaculately modernized eighteenth-century house, complete with a string of period features, this lovely place has three rooms: two suites (for up to five guests) and a single room in the courtyard-garden. The location is handy, near the castle.

AT GENESIS MAP P.96, POCKET MAP C12. Hertogstraat 15 ☎ 0486 14 10 25, ⓦ stayatgenesis.com. Doubles from €100. In the heart of the Patershol, in a sympathetically modernized old terrace house, this B&B offers two second-floor guest rooms – one for two guests; the other for six – located above an artist's studio. Both come with a kitchenette and have lots of nice decorative touches and beamed ceilings.

SIMON SAYS MAP P.96, POCKET MAP C11. Sluizeken 8 ☎ 09 233 03 43, ⓦ simon-says.be. Doubles from €130. On the edge of the Patershol, in a good-looking building with an Art Nouveau facade, this combined coffee bar and B&B has just two guest rooms, both fairly small and straightforwardly modern, en-suite affairs.

The breakfasts are splendid and reasonably priced – be sure to try the croissants.

DE WATERZOOI MAP P.96, POCKET MAP B12. St-Veerleplein 2 ☎ 0475 43 61 11, wdewaterzooi.be. Doubles from €170. Superbly renovated eighteenth-century mansion with a handful of handsome rooms that manage to make the most of their antique setting but are extraordinarily comfortable at the same time – the split-level attic room is the most ambitious. There are wonderful views of the castle, and if the weather is good you can take breakfast outside in the garden-patio. Minimum two- or sometimes three-night stay at peak periods.

Hostels in Ghent

HOSTEL 47 MAP P.96, POCKET MAP E11. Blekerijstraat 47 ☎ 0478 71 28 27, ⓦ hostel47.com. Dorm beds from €27, doubles from €66. Well-kept hostel with spacious and clean two- to six-bed dormitories in an old house about a fifteen-minute walk from the city centre. There's a small garden and shared bathrooms. A basic breakfast is included in the price.

JEUGDHERBERG DE DRAECKE MAP P.96, POCKET MAP B12. St-Widostraat 11 ☎ 09 233 70 50, ⓦ jeugdherbergen.be. Dorm beds from €28, doubles from €62. Well-equipped, HI-affiliated hostel that's just a five-minute walk north of the Korenmarkt. Has 120 beds in two- to six-bunk, en-suite rooms, plus a library, bar and lounge. Advance reservations are advised, especially in summer. Breakfast included.

UPPELINK HOSTEL MAP P.96, POCKET MAP B13. St-Michielsplein 21 ☎ 09 279 44 77, ⓦ hostelworld.com. Dorm beds from €12, doubles from €40. A family-owned hostel in a prime location, occupying a rambling late-nineteenth-century building right beside St-Michielsbrug. Some of the rooms have great views over the city centre and the public areas are a fetching mix of antique fittings and boho-distressed furnishings. Laundry facilities; free luggage storage and kayak rental (single kayak €16 for 3 hours, twin kayak €13 for 3 hours per person). Dorms have between six and fourteen bunk beds. Minimum two-night stay during summer.

ESSENTIALS

Cycling in Bruges

Arrival

Bruges and Ghent are easy to reach by road and rail. The **E40 motorway**, linking Brussels with Ostend, runs just south of both cities and there are fast and frequent **trains** to Ghent and Bruges from Brussels and a batch of other Belgian cities. Long-distance **international buses** also run direct to Bruges and Ghent from a number of capital cities, including London with Eurolines, and there are **car ferries** from Hull to Zeebrugge, near Bruges. The nearest airport to both cities is Brussels. There are three trains an hour between Bruges and Ghent; the journey time between the two is about twenty minutes.

In **Bruges**, the train and bus station are next to one another, about 2km southwest of the city centre. If the flat and easy twenty-minute walk into the centre doesn't appeal, local bus #12 departs for the main square, the Markt, from outside the train station every few minutes; other services stop on the Markt or in the surrounding side streets. All local buses have destination signs at the front, but if in doubt check with the driver. A taxi from the train station to the centre should cost about €12.

Ghent has three train stations, but the one you're almost certain to arrive at is Ghent St-Pieters, which adjoins the main bus station some 2km south of the city centre. From outside the train station, Tram #1 (destination Evergem, NOT Flanders Expo) runs up to the Korenmarkt at the heart of the city every few minutes. All trams have destination signs and numbers at the front, but if in doubt check with the driver. The taxi fare from the train station to the Korenmarkt is about €12.

By air

The nearest airport to Bruges and Ghent is **Brussels international airport**. From the airport, there are three or four trains every hour to Brussels' three main stations: **Bruxelles-Nord, Bruxelles-Centrale** and **Bruxelles-Midi**. The journey time to Bruxelles-Nord is about twenty minutes; a few minutes more to the others. You can change at any of these stations for the twice-hourly train from Brussels to Bruges and Ghent, though changing at Bruxelles-Nord is a tad more convenient since it isn't usually as crowded as the other two. The journey from Brussels takes an hour to Bruges, thirty-five minutes to Ghent. There are also direct trains from the airport to Ghent (1–2 hourly), from where there are onward connections to Bruges (3 hourly; 20min), but this isn't much quicker. The one-way fare from Brussels' airport to Bruges is currently €21.60, twice that for a return; the fare to Ghent is slightly less. Note that some flights to Brussels (including Ryanair) land at **Brussels South Charleroi** airport, well to the south of the capital and an hour or so away from Brussels by airport bus.

By train

Bruges and Ghent are extremely well served by train (ⓦ belgianrail. be), with fast and frequent services from a number of Belgian towns and cities including Brussels and Ostend. Trains from Brussels to Bruges and Ghent depart from all three of the capital's mainline stations including Bruxelles-Midi, the terminus of Eurostar trains from London. **Eurostar** trains (ⓦ eurostar.com) take two hours to get from London St Pancras to Bruxelles-Midi station, from where it's another hour or so by domestic train to get to Bruges, forty minutes to Ghent; there's through-ticketing with Eurostar too. Bruxelles-Midi station

City passes

In **Bruges**, a splurge of new (and occasionally tawdry) attractions made Bruges's old CityCard pass increasingly hard to co-ordinate and as a consequence it was abandoned in 2016. It may or may not be revived, but in the meantime the best you'll do is the **Museum Pass** (see page 29), which is valid for three days, covers entry to all the main museums and costs €20 (12–25-year-olds €15; Ⓦ visitbruges.be/practical-information). In **Ghent**, on the other hand, the money-saving **CityCard Gent** covers all the key attractions, provides free and unlimited use of the city's buses and trams and includes a boat trip and a day's bike rental; it costs €30 for 48hr, €35 for 72hr. It's on sale at any of the participants as well as from tourist information centres (see page 145).

is also served by **Thalys** (Ⓦ thalys.com) international express trains from Amsterdam, Cologne, Aachen and Paris.

By car

To reach Belgium by car or motorbike from the UK, you can either take the Hull-Zeebrugge car ferry (see below) or use **Eurotunnel's shuttle train** through the Channel Tunnel from near Folkestone (exit the M20 at junction 11a). Note that Eurotunnel only carries cars (including occupants) and motorbikes, not cyclists and foot passengers. From the Eurotunnel exit in Calais, it's just 120km to Bruges and 200km to Brussels.

Bruges is clearly signed from the E40 motorway, and its oval-shaped centre is encircled by the R30 ring road, which follows the course of the old city walls. **Parking** in the centre can be a real tribulation, with on-street parking almost impossible to find and the city centre's handful of car parks often filled to the gunnels. Easily the best option is to use the massive

24/7 car park by the train station, particularly as the price – €3.50 per day – includes the cost of the bus ride to and from the centre.

Ghent is also well signed from the E40 motorway and encircled by a ring road. There are free P+R **car parks** on the edge of town and a dozen or so large and metered car parks within the city centre – reckon on €26 for a 24hr stay, around €11 for 6 hours. The 24-hour car park beneath the Vrijdagmarkt is one of the best placed.

By ferry

At time of writing, there is only one **car ferry** operating between the UK and Belgium. This links Hull and Zeebrugge, a few kilometres from Bruges, and is operated by **P&O Ferries** (Ⓦ poferries.com); the sailing time is around 13hr. Tariffs vary enormously, depending on when you leave, how long you stay, what size your vehicle is and how many passengers are in it; there's also the cost of a cabin to consider.

Getting around

By bus and tram

Local buses in Bruges and buses and trams in Ghent are all operated by

De Lijn (☎ 070 22 02 00, Ⓦ delijn.be) with a standard one-way fare costing €3. Tickets are valid for an hour and can be purchased at automatic ticket machines and from the driver. A 24-hour city transport pass, the **Dagpas**, costs €6 (€8 from the driver). In both cities, there's a **De Lijn information kiosk** outside the train station and they issue free maps of the transport system – as does tourist information (see page 145). Note also that a **Ghent city pass** (see page 139) includes public transport.

By bike

Flat as a pair of pancakes, Bruges and Ghent are great places to cycle, especially as there are cycle lanes on many of the roads and cycle racks dotted across both city centres. In Bruges, there are about a dozen bike rental places – tourist information has the full list. The largest is **Fietspunt Brugge**, beside the train station (April–Sept Mon–Fri 7am–7pm, Sat & Sun 10am–9pm; Oct–March Mon–Fri 7am–7pm; ☎ 050 39 68 26) and here, a standard-issue bike costs €15 per day (€4 an hour), plus a refundable deposit of €10. In Ghent, bike rental is available at St-Pieters train station with the **Blue-bike scheme** (☎ 09 241 22 24; registration €10 & €3 per hour) and from **Biker**, on the northeast side of the city centre at Steendam 16 (Tues–Sat 9am–12.30pm & 1.30–6pm; ☎ 09 224 29 03, ⊛ bikerfietsen.be); for a standard bike, Biker charges €9 per day.

By canal boat

Throughout the season, canal trips explore **Ghent**'s inner waterways, departing from the Korenlei quay, just near the Korenmarkt, as well as from the Vleeshuisbrug, beside the Kraanlei (April–Oct daily 10am–6pm; €7). Trips last forty minutes and leave every fifteen minutes or so, though the wait can be longer as boats often delay their departure until they are reasonably full. Similarly, in **Bruges**, there are canal trips along the city's central canals with boats departing from a number of jetties south of the Burg (March–Nov daily 10am–6pm; €8). Boats leave every few minutes, but long queues can still build up; in winter (Dec–Feb), there's a spasmodic service at weekends only. There are also boat excursions out from Bruges to the attractive little town of **Damme** (see page 88)

By horse-drawn carriage

In Ghent, horse-drawn carriages, which can hold a maximum of five, congregate outside the Lakenhalle, offering a thirty-minute canter round town for €35 (Easter to Oct daily 10am–6pm & most winter weekends). In Bruges, horse-drawn carriages line up on the Markt (daily 10am–10pm; €50 per carriage) to offer a 30min canter around the town centre; demand can outstrip supply, so expect to queue at the weekend.

By guided tour

In Ghent, there are several different types of guided walking tour to choose from, but the standard tour, operated by city's **Guides' Association**, is a two-hour jaunt around the city centre (May–Sept 1 daily, Oct–March Sat & Sun 1 daily; tours start at 2pm; €10); they include a visit to either the Stadhuis (Mon–Fri) or the Cathedral (Sat & Sun). Tickets are on sale at tourist information (see page 145) and advance booking – at least a few hours ahead of time – is strongly recommended. In Bruges, there is a bewildering range of guided tours to choose from – beer, scooter, minibus and so forth – and tourist information (see page 145) has the full list. One of the better options is the "**Bruges by Heart**" guided walking tour organised by the city's Guides' Association (April–Sept at least 1 weekly; 2hr;

Mosquitoes

These pesky blighters thrive in the canals of Bruges and Ghent and can be a real handful (or mouthful). An antihistamine cream such as Phenergan is the best antidote, although this can be difficult to find – in which case preventative sticks like Autan or Citronella are the best bet.

€12.50); advance booking is strongly recommended.

By guided cycling tour

In Bruges, **Quasimundo** (☏ 050 33 07 75, ⓦ quasimundo.com) runs several cycling tours, starting from the Burg. Their "Bruges by Bike" excursion (March–Oct 1 daily; 2.5hr; €28) zips round the main sights and then explores less-visited parts of the city, while their "Border by Bike" tour (March–Oct 1 daily; 4hr; €28) is a 25km ride out along the poplar-lined canals to the northeast of Bruges, visiting Damme and Oostkerke

along the way. The price includes mountain-bike and rain-jacket hire; reservations are required.

By taxi

Bruges has several taxi ranks, including one on the Markt and another outside the train station. Fares are metered – and the most common journey, from the train station to the centre, costs about €12; Bruges to Damme costs about €20. Similarly, Ghent has a number of taxi ranks, including one outside the train station; a taxi from Ghent train station to the centre should cost about €12.

Entry requirements

Citizens of the EU (European Union) and EEA (European Economic Area), including the UK (at least until "Brexit", when Britain leaves the EU) and Ireland, plus citizens of Australia, New Zealand, Canada and the US do not need a visa to enter Belgium if staying for ninety days or less, but they do need a current passport (or EU national identity card), whose validity exceeds the length of their stay by at least three months. Travellers from South Africa, on the other hand, need a passport and a tourist visa for visits of less than ninety days; visas must be obtained before departure and are available from the appropriate embassy (see below). For stays of longer than ninety days, EU/EEA residents will have few problems, but everyone else needs a mix of visas and permits. In all cases,

consult the appropriate embassy at home before departure.

Belgian embassies abroad

For further information, consult ⓦ diplomatie.belgium.be/en
Australia ⓦ australia.diplomatie.belgium.be/en
Canada ⓦ canada.diplomatie.belgium.be/en
Ireland ⓦ ireland.diplomatie.belgium.be/en
Luxembourg ⓦ luxembourg.diplomatie.belgium.be
New Zealand No embassy – see Australia – but there is consular representation in Wellington.
South Africa ⓦ southafrica.diplomatie.belgium.be/en
UK ⓦ unitedkingdom.diplomatie.belgium.be/en
US ⓦ unitedstates.diplomatie.belgium.be/en

Directory A–Z

Addresses

In Flemish-speaking Belgium, the first line of the address gives the name of the street which is followed by (and joined to) its category – hence Krakeelplein is Krakeel square, Krakeelstraat is Krakeel street; the number comes next. The second line gives the area – or zip – code followed by the town or area. Consequently, Flemish abbreviations occur at the end of words: thus Hofstr for Hofstraat. An exception is Grote Markt (main square), which is not abbreviated.

Cinema

Films are normally shown in the original language, with Dutch subtitles as required. In **Bruges**, the Cinema Lumière St-Jacobstraat 36 (☎ 050 34 34 65, ⓦ lumierecinema.be) is the premier venue for alternative, cult, foreign and art-house movies, with three screens. In **Ghent**, the Sphinx (Sint-Michielshelling 3 ☎ 09 225 60 86, ⓦ sphinx-cinema.be), focuses on foreign-language and art-house films (with original soundtrack); Studio Skoop (St-Annaplein 63 ☎ 09 225 08 45, ⓦ studioskoop.be) is the cosiest of the city's cinemas, but still with five screens.

Crime and personal safety

Ghent and Bruges are relatively free of crime, though it's always advisable to guard against petty theft. If you are robbed, you'll need to go to the police to report it, not least because your insurance company will require a police report; remember to make a note of the report number – or, better still, ask for a copy of the statement itself. As for personal safety, it's generally possible to walk around without fear of harassment or assault, but certain parts of Ghent require a little caution.

Electricity

The current is 220 volts AC, with standard European-style two-pin plugs. British equipment needs only a plug adaptor; American apparatus requires a transformer and an adaptor.

Football

Both Ghent and Bruges have top-flight football (soccer) teams. They are Club Brugge (ⓦ clubbrugge.be), who often win the league, and KAA Gent (ⓦ kaagent.be), who rarely win anything. The former play at the Jan Breydel Stadion, about 5km southwest of Bruges city centre; the latter play at the Ghelamco Arena, about 6km south of Ghent city centre. There are buses to the stadiums from both city train stations.

Gay and lesbian scene

The gay and lesbian scene in Ghent and more especially Bruges is distinctly low key. The legal framework, however, is notably progressive with, for example, same-sex marriages legalised in Belgium in 2003. The age of consent for men and women is 16.

Health and insurance

Under reciprocal health care arrangements, all citizens of the **EU** and **EEA** are entitled to free, or at least subsidized, **medical treatment** within Belgium's public health care system. With the exception of **Australians**, whose government has a reciprocal health agreement with Belgium, **non-**

Emergency number

For police, fire & emergency medical assistance, call ☎ 112.

ATMs in Bruges and Ghent

Bruges: There are central ATMs at Europabank, Vlamingstraat 13, and ING, just off the Markt at St-Amandstraat 13. There are also ATMs at the train station.

Ghent: ING has ATMs at most of its branches, including Belfortstraat 18, and Europabank has an ATM at their branch on the Groentenmarkt.

EU/EEA nationals are not entitled to any free treatment and should, therefore, take out their own medical insurance. However, EU/EEA citizens may also want to consider private health insurance, both to cover the cost of items not within the EU/EEA scheme, such as dental treatment and repatriation on medical grounds, and to enable them to seek treatment within the private sector. Note also that the more worthwhile insurance policies promise to sort matters out before you pay (rather than after) in the case of major expense; if you do have to pay upfront, get and keep the receipts. No inoculations are currently required for Belgium.

If you're seeking treatment under EU/ EEA reciprocal health arrangements, it may be necessary to double-check that the medic you see is working within (and seeing you as) a patient of the public system. That being the case, you'll receive subsidized treatment just as the locals do. Technically you should have your passport and your **European Health Insurance Card (EHIC)** to hand to prove that you are eligible for EU/EEA health care, but often no one bothers to check. English-speaking medical staff are commonplace. Your hotel will usually be able to arrange – or help to arrange – an appointment with a doctor/ dentist, but note that he/she will almost certainly see you as a private patient.

Finally, minor ailments can often be remedied at a **pharmacy** (*apotheek*): pharmacists are highly trained, willing to give advice and able to dispense many drugs which would only be available on prescription in many other countries. Pharmacies are ubiquitous and late-night duty rotas are usually displayed in every pharmacist's window.

Money

In Belgium, the currency is the **euro** (€). Each euro is made up of 100 cents. There are seven euro notes – in denominations of €500, €200, €100, €50, €20, €10 and €5 – and eight different **coins**, specifically €2 and €1, then 50, 20, 10, 5, 2 and 1 cents. Euro notes and coins feature a common EU design on one face, but different country-specific designs on the other. Note that many retailers will not touch the €500 and €200 notes with a bargepole – you have to break them down into smaller denominations at the bank. At the time of writing the **rate of exchange** for €1 is £0.86; US$1.23; Can$1.55; Aus$1.59; NZ$1.68; ZAR14.85. For the most up-to-date rates, check the currency converter website ⓦ oanda.com.

ATMs are liberally distributed across both Bruges and Ghent – and they accept a host of debit cards without charging a transaction fee. Credit cards can be used in ATMs too, but in this case transactions are treated as loans, with interest accruing daily from the date of withdrawal. All major **credit/ debit cards** are widely accepted in both cities. Typically, ATMs give instructions in a variety of languages.

You can change **foreign currency** into Euros at most banks, which are ubiquitous; **banking hours** are usually Monday to Friday from 9am to 3.30/4pm, with a few banks also open on Saturday mornings.

Opening hours

Business hours (ie office hours) normally run from Monday to Friday 9.30/10am to 4.30/5pm. Normal **shopping hours** are Monday through Saturday 10am to 5.30/6pm, though many smaller shops open late on Monday morning and/or close a tad earlier on Saturdays. At the other extreme, larger establishments – primarily supermarkets and department stores – are very likely to have extended hours, often on Fridays when many remain open till 9pm and/or on Sundays, normally 10am–5pm. Both Bruges and Ghent also have a smattering of **convenience stores** (*avondwinkels*), which stay open either all night or until 1/2am daily. In Belgium, there are ten national **public holidays** per year and two regional/provincial holidays (see page 146). For the most part, these holidays are keenly observed, with most businesses and many attractions closed and public transport reduced to a Sunday service.

Phones

All but the remotest parts of Belgium are on the **mobile phone (cell phone)** network at GSM900/1800, the band common to the rest of Europe, Australia and New Zealand. Mobile/cell phones bought in North America will need to be able to adjust to this GSM band. If you intend to use your own mobile/cell phone in Belgium, you may want to check call rates with your supplier before you depart. You may find it cheaper to buy a **local SIM card**, though this can get complicated: many mobiles/cells will not permit you to swap SIM cards and the connection instructions for the replacement SIM card may not be in English. If you overcome these problems, you can buy local SIM cards at high-street phone companies, which offer myriad deals beginning at about €5 per SIM card.

There are **no area codes**, but Belgian numbers mostly begin with a zero, a relic of former area codes, which

---

Useful telephone numbers

Operator numbers

Domestic directory enquiries: Flemish ☎ 1207; French ☎ 1307. **International directory enquiries & operator assistance Flemish**: ☎ 1204; **French** ☎ 1304.

International calls

To make an international phone call from Belgium, dial the appropriate international access code as below, then the number you require, omitting the initial zero where there is one.
Australia ☎ 0061
Canada ☎ 001
Republic of Ireland ☎ 00353
New Zealand ☎ 0064
South Africa ☎ 0027
UK ☎ 0044
US ☎ 001

Phoning Belgium from abroad

To call Belgium from abroad, dial your international access code, then ☎ 32 (the country code for Belgium), followed by the subscriber number minus its initial zero where there is one.

have now been incorporated into the numbers themselves. Telephone numbers beginning ☎ 0900 or ☎ 070 are premium-rated, ☎ 0800 are toll-free. There's no distinction between local and long-distance calls – in other words calling Ostend from Bruges costs the same as calling a number in Brussels.

Post

Belgium has an efficient postal system with its **post boxes** painted red. Mail to the US takes seven days or so, within Europe two to three days. **Post offices** are now thin on the ground, but stamps are sold at a wide range of outlets including many shops and hotels. The main post office in Bruges is well to the west of the city centre at Smedenstraat 57 (Mon–Fri 9am–6pm, Sat 9am–3pm); in Ghent, the main post office is at Lange Kruisstraat 55 (Mon–Fri 9am–6pm, Sat 9am–3pm).

Time

Belgium is on **Central European Time (CET)**, one hour ahead of Greenwich Mean Time, six hours ahead of US Eastern Standard Time, nine hours ahead of US Pacific Standard Time, nine hours behind Australian Eastern Standard Time, and eleven hours behind New Zealand. There are, however, minor variations during the changeover periods involved in **daylight saving**.

Tipping

There's no need to tip when there's a **service charge** – as there often is – but when there isn't, restaurant waiters will anticipate a ten to fifteen percent gratuity. In **taxis**, passengers will simply round up the fare.

Toilets

Public toilets are comparatively rare, but some cafés and bars run what amounts to an ablutionary sideline, with an attendant keeping the toilets scrupulously clean and making a minimal charge. Where it still applies, you'll spot the plate for the money as you enter.

Tourist information

In **Bruges**, there are three **tourist information offices**: a small one at the train station (daily 10am–5pm); the main one in the Concertgebouw (Concert Hall) complex, on the west side of the city centre on 't Zand (Mon–Sat 10am–5pm, Sun 10am–2pm); and a third on the Markt (daily 10am–5pm), in the same building as the Historium. They have a common phone line and website (☎ 050 44 46 46, ⊛ visitbruges.be).

Ghent's tourist office is located in the Oude Vismijn, opposite the castle on St-Veerleplein (mid-March to mid-Oct daily 10am–6pm; mid-Oct to mid-March 9.30am–4.30pm; ☎ 09 266 56 60, ⊛ visit.gent.be).

Travelling with children

Belgian society is generally sympathetic to its children and the tourist industry follows suit. Extra beds in hotel rooms are usually easy to arrange; many restaurants (but not the smartest) have children's menus; concessions for children are the rule, from public transport to museums; and baby-changing stations are commonplace. Pharmacists carry all the kiddy stuff you would expect – nappies, baby food and so forth – and a few hotels offer a babysitting service.

Travellers with disabilities

The most obvious difficulty facing people with **mobility problems** is in negotiating the cobbled streets and narrow, often broken pavements of the older districts, where the key sights are mostly located. Similarly, provision for people with disabilities on the **public transport system** is only average, although improving – many new buses, for instance, are now wheelchair accessible. And yet, while it can be difficult simply to get around, practically all **public buildings**, including museums, theatres, cinemas, concert halls and hotels, are obliged to provide access, and do. Hotels and hostels that have been certified wheelchair-accessible carry the **International Accessibility Symbol (ISA)**. Bear in mind, however, that a lot of the older, narrower hotels are not allowed to install lifts for reasons of conservation, so check first.

Festivals and events

Bruges and Ghent are big on festivals and special events – everything from religious processions through to cinema, fairs and contemporary musical binges – and we have listed a selection below. Information on upcoming festivals and events is easy to come by from tourist information and their websites (see page 145).

Late April to mid-May

Meifoor (Bruges) Late April to mid-May; Ⓦ visitbruges.be. Bruges's main annual funfair, held on 't Zand and in the adjoining Koning Albertpark.

May

Festival van Vlaanderen (Flanders Festival) (Bruges & Ghent) May–Oct across Flanders; Ⓦ festival.be. For well over forty years, the Flanders Festival has provided classical music in churches, castles and other impressive venues in over sixty Flemish towns and cities. The festival now comprises more than 120 concerts and features international orchestras. Each of the big Dutch-speaking cities – including Ghent and Bruges – gets a fair crack of the cultural whip, with the festival celebrated for about two weeks in each city before it moves on to the next.

Heilig Bloedprocessie (Procession of the Holy Blood) (Bruges) Ascension Day (forty days after Easter); Ⓦ visitbruges.be. One of medieval Christendom's holiest relics, the phial of the Holy Blood is carried through the centre of Bruges once annually. Nowadays, the procession is as much a tourist attraction as a religious ceremony, but it remains an important event for many citizens of Bruges.

July

Cactusfestival (Bruges) Three days over the second weekend of July; Ⓦ cactusfestival.be. Going strong for over twenty years, the Cactusfestival is

Public holidays in Flanders

New Year's Day
Easter Monday
Labour Day (May 1)
Ascension Day (forty days after Easter)
Whit Monday
Flemish Day (Flemish-speaking Belgium only; July 11)
Belgium National Day (July 21)
Assumption (mid-August)
All Saints' Day (November 1)
Armistice Day (November 11)
Christmas Day
(Note that if any of the above falls on a Sunday, the next day becomes a holiday).

Major venues

Bruges

CONCERTGEBOUW
MAP P.48, POCKET MAP B7

't Zand 34 ☏ 050 47 69 99, ticket line ☏ 070 22 33 02, ⓦ concertgebouw.be.
Outstanding concert hall, built in 2002 and now hosting all the
performing arts, from opera and classical music through to big-name
bands. Offers enjoyable 50-minute guided tours too (€8).

STADSSCHOUWBURG
MAP P.72, POCKET MAP C5

Vlamingstraat 29 ☏ 050 44 30 60, ⓦ ccbrugge.be.
Occupying a big neo-Renaissance building from 1869, and with a
wide-ranging programme, including theatre, dance, musicals, concerts
and opera.

Ghent

CONCERTZAAL HANDELSBEURS
MAP P.96, POCKET MAP C14

Kouter 29 ☏ 09 265 91 60, ⓦ handelsbeurs.be.
The city's primary concert hall with two auditoria and hosting a wide
and diverse programme.

MUZIEKCENTRUM DE BIJLOKE
MAP P.122, POCKET MAP B16

Godhuizenlaan 2 ☏ 09 323 61 00, ⓦ bijloke.be.
The old Bijloke abbey complex now holds the STAM historical
museum (see page 119) and a Muziekcentrum, which includes a
smart new Concert Hall.

NT GENT SCHOUWBURG
MAP P.96, POCKET MAP C13

St-Baafsplein 17 ☏ 09 225 01 01, ⓦ ntgent.be.
Municipal theatre accommodating the Nederlands Toneel Gent, the
regional repertory company. Most of their performances are in Flemish,
though they do host touring English-language theatre companies.

VLAAMSE OPERA GENT
MAP P.96, POCKET MAP C14

Schouwburgstraat 3 ☏ 070 22 02 02, ⓦ operaballet.be.
Handsomely restored nineteenth-century opera house, where the
city's opera company performs when not on tour.

VOORUIT
MAP P.122 POCKET MAP D15

St-Pietersnieuwstraat 23 ☏ 09 267 28 28, ⓦ vooruit.be.
Leading venue for rock, pop and jazz (see page 121).

something of a classic. Known for its
amiable atmosphere, it proudly pushes
against the musical mainstream with
rock, reggae, rap, roots and R&B all
rolling along together. The festival
features both domestic and foreign
artists. It's held in Bruges's city centre,
in the park beside the Minnewater.

Gentse Feesten (Ghent Festival)
Mid- to late July, but always including July 21; ⓦ gentsefeesten.stad.gent. For ten days every July, Ghent gets stuck into partying pretty much round the clock. Local bands perform free open-air gigs throughout the city and street performers turn up all over the place. There's also an outdoor market selling everything from *jenever* (gin) to handmade crafts.

Moods (Bruges) Two and a half weeks, usually from the last weekend of July; ⓦ moodsbrugge.be. Bruges's biggest annual knees-up, and the chance for city folk to let their hair down. There are big-time concerts on the Markt and the Burg, the city's two main squares, more intimate performances in various bars and cafés, plus all sorts of other entertainments. It's Bruges at its best – and most of the events are free.

Musica Antiqua (Bruges) Four days in early Aug; ⓦ mafestival.be. Part of the Festival van Vlaanderen (see page 146), this well-established and well-regarded festival of medieval music offers an extensive programme of live performances at a variety of venues in Bruges. The evening concerts are built around themes, whilst the lunchtime concerts are more episodic. Tickets go on sale in Feb and are snapped up fast.

August

Praalstoet van de Gouden Boom (Pageant of the Golden Tree) (Bruges) Held every five years over two days on the last weekend of August, this pageant features all sorts of mock-medieval heartiness, and thousands congregate in central Bruges to join in the fun. First staged in 1958, the next one is due in 2022.

October

Ghent Film Festival (Ghent). Eleven days in October; ⓦ filmfestival.be. This is one of Europe's foremost cinematic events in which the city's cinemas (see page 142) combine to present a total of around two hundred feature films and a hundred shorts from all over the world. Many films are screened long before they hit the international circuit. There's also a special focus on music in film.

December

The Arrival of St Nicholas (aka Santa Klaus) (Bruges and Ghent) Dec 6. The arrival of St Nicholas from his long sojourn abroad is celebrated by processions and the giving of sweets to children right across Belgium.

Kerstmarkt (Christmas Market) (Bruges). Dec daily 11am–10pm. Bruges' Christmas Market occupies the Markt with scores of brightly lit stalls selling food, drink, souvenirs and everything Christmassy. Part of the Markt is also turned into an ice rink – and you can rent skates.

Chronology

630 The French missionary St Amand establishes an abbey on the site of present-day Ghent, at the confluence of the rivers Leie and Scheldt.

865 Bruges founded as a coastal stronghold against the Vikings by the splendidly named Baldwin Iron Arm, first count of Flanders.

Tenth century The beginnings of the wool industry in Flanders. The leading Flemish cloth towns are Bruges and Ghent.

Twelfth to late-fourteenth century The Flemish cloth industry becomes dependent on English wool. Flanders enjoys an unprecedented economic boom and its merchants become immensely rich. However, there is increasing tension – and bouts of warfare – between the merchants and weavers of Flanders, for whom friendship with England is vital, and their feudal overlords, the counts of Flanders, who are vassals of England's traditional enemy, the kings of France. Ghent becomes the seat of the counts of Flanders and the largest town in western Europe.

1302 A dreadful year for France. In May, during the Bruges Matins, the citizens of Bruges massacre the French garrison that had been billeted upon them: anyone who couldn't correctly pronounce the Flemish shibboleth schild en vriend ("shield and friend") was put to the sword. In July, at the Battle of the Golden Spurs, the Flemish militia defeat the French army, slaughtering hundreds of heavily armoured knights

1384 The dukes of Burgundy inherit Flanders.

1419 Philip the Good, Duke of Burgundy, makes Bruges his capital. The Burgundian court becomes known across Europe for its cultured opulence – and the elongated, pointy shoes of its male courtiers. Philip dies in 1467.

1482 Mary, the last of the Burgundians, dies and her territories – including Flanders – revert to her husband, Maximilian, a Habsburg prince. Thus, Flanders is absorbed into the Habsburg empire.

1480s onwards Decline of the Flemish cloth industry.

1530s Bruges's international trade collapses and the town slips into a long decline. Ghent also experiences a decline, though its merchants switch from industry to trade, keeping the city going – if not exactly flourishing.

Mid-sixteenth to seventeenth century The Protestants of the Low Countries (modern-day Belgium and the Netherlands) rebel against their Catholic Habsburg rulers. A long and cruel series of wars ensues. Eventually, the Netherlands wins its independence – as the United Provinces – but the south, including Flanders, fails to escape the Habsburgs and is reconstituted as the Spanish Netherlands.

1700 The last of the Spanish Habsburgs, Charles II, dies; the War of the Spanish Succession follows.

1713 The Treaty of Utrecht cedes what is now Belgium, including Flanders, to the Austrians – as the Austrian Netherlands.

1794 Napoleon occupies the Austrian Netherlands and annexes it to France the following year.

1815 Napoleon is defeated at Waterloo, near Brussels, and the Austrian Netherlands becomes half of the new 'Kingdom of The Netherlands'.

1830 A rebellion leads to the collapse of the new kingdom and the creation of an independent Belgium, including Flanders.

Mid- to late-nineteenth century Much of Belgium industrializes, including Ghent but not Bruges, whose antique charms attract a first wave of tourists.

1913 The Great Exhibition, showing the best in contemporary design and goods, is staged in Ghent.

1914–1945 The Germans occupy Bruges and Ghent in both world wars. The cities themselves remain largely unscathed, but many citizens are not so lucky. Some Belgians collaborate and post-war retribution follows:

56,000 alleged Belgian collaborators are prosecuted, 250 executed.

Late 1940s to 1950s Historic tensions between the French- and Dutch-speaking regions of Belgium augment and ferment.

1962 Entrenching animosities: creation of the Belgian "Language Frontier" distinguishing French- from Flemish-speaking Belgium.

1980 More communal entrenchment: Belgium adopts a federal form of government with three regions – the Flemish north, Walloon (French-speaking) south and bilingual Brussels. Dutch-speaking Flanders includes the two provinces of East and West Flanders (Ghent is in East Flanders, Bruges in West).

1990 A right royal pantomime when Catholic King Baudouin abdicates for the day while the law legalizing abortion is ratified.

2002 Out with the Belgian franc – in with the euro.

2003 Belgium becomes the second country in the world to legalize same-sex marriage.

2010 Political failure: after Belgium's federal elections in 2010, it takes more than a year to create a ruling coalition amidst much Walloon/Flemish disputation. There is a repeat performance four years later – but this time the interregnum lasts for five months. The Flemish Parliament carries on pretty much regardless.

2014 In regional elections, the New Flemish Alliance (N-VA; Nieuw-Vlaamse Alliantie) cements its position as the largest party in Flanders, which is bad news for anyone on the left: the N-VA is conservative, nationalistic and committed to the secession of Flanders from Belgium.

2016 Savage jihadist attack on Brussels' airport with 35 killed – the worst of several outrages this year and the year after.

2018 Embarrassments galore: the Belgian army much mocked for its plans to allow homesick recruits to sleep at home rather than in barracks; Prince Laurent, the younger brother of King Philippe, has his federal allowance reduced after a series of mistakes, which have earnt him the nickname the écolo-gaffeur (eco-blunderer).

Language

Throughout the northern part of Belgium, including West and East Flanders – which covers Bruges and Ghent – the principal language is Dutch, which is spoken in a variety of distinctive dialects commonly described as "Flemish". Dutch-speaking Belgians commonly refer to themselves as Flemish-speakers and most of them, particularly in the tourist industry, also speak English to varying degrees of excellence. Indeed, Flemish-speakers have a seemingly natural talent for languages, and your attempts at speaking theirs may be met with bewilderment – though this can have as much to do with your pronunciation (Dutch/Flemish is very difficult to get right) as surprise that you're making the effort.

Consequently, the following words and phrases should be the most you'll need to get by. We've also included a basic **food and drink** glossary, though menus are nearly always multilingual; where they aren't, ask and one will almost invariably appear.

As for **phrasebooks**, the pocket-sized *Rough Guide to Dutch* has a good dictionary section (English–Dutch and Dutch–English) as well as a menu reader; it also provides a useful introduction to grammar and pronunciation.

Pronunciation

Dutch is **pronounced** much the same as English, though there are a few Dutch sounds that don't exist in English and which can be difficult to get right without practice.

Consonants

j is an English **y**, as in **y**ellow
ch and **g** indicate a throaty sound, as at the end of the Scottish word loch. The Dutch word for canal – *gracht* – is especially tricky, since it has two of these sounds – it comes out sounding something like *khrakht*. A common word for hello is *Dag!* – pronounced like *daakh*
ng as in bring
nj as in onion
y is not a consonant, but another way of writing ij
Double-consonant combinations generally keep their separate sounds in Flemish: **kn**, for example, is never like the English "knight".

Vowels and diphthongs

A good rule of thumb is that doubling the letter lengthens the vowel sound.
a is like the English **a**pple
aa like c**a**rt
e like l**e**t
ee like l**a**te
o as in p**o**p
oo in p**o**pe
u is like the French t**u** if preceded by a consonant; it's like w**oo**d if followed by a consonant
uu is like the French t**u**
au and **ou** like h**ow**
ei and **ij** as in f**i**ne, though this varies strongly from region to region; sometimes it can sound more like l**a**ne
oe as in s**oo**n
eu is like the diphthong in the French l**eu**r
ui is the hardest Dutch diphthong of all,

pronounced like h**ow** but much further forward in the mouth, with lips pursed (as if to say "oo").

Words and phrases

Basic expressions

ja yes
nee no
alstublieft please
dank u or bedankt thank you
hallo or dag hello
goedemorgen good morning
goedemiddag good afternoon
goedenavond good evening
tot ziens goodbye
tot straks see you later
Spreekt u Engels? Do you speak English?
Ik begrijp het niet I don't understand
vrouwen/mannen women/men
kinderen children
heren/dames men's/women's toilets
Ik wil... I want...
Ik wil niet... I don't want to...**(+verb)**
Ik wil geen... I don't want any...**(+noun)**
Wat kost...? How much is...?
sorry sorry
hier/daar here/there
goed/slecht good/bad
groot/klein big/small
open/gesloten open/closed
duwen/trekken push/pull
nieuw/oud new/old
goedkoop/duur cheap/expensive
heet or warm/koud hot/cold
met/zonder with/without
Hoe kom ik in...? How do I get to...?
Waar is...? Where is...?
Hoe ver is het How far is it to...? **naar...?**
Wanneer? When?
ver/dichtbij far/near
links/rechts left/right
rechtdoor straight ahead
alle richtingen all directions (road sign)
postkantoor post office
postzegel(s) stamp(s)
geldwisselkantoor money exchange
kassa cash desk
spoor or perron railway platform
loket ticket office

Useful cycling terms

fiets Bicycle
fietspad bicycle path
band tyre
lek puncture
rem brake
ketting chain
wiel wheel
trapper pedal
pomp pump
stuur handlebars
kapot broken

Numbers

nul 0
een 1
twee 2
drie 3
vier 4
vijf 5
zes 6
zeven 7
acht 8
negen 9
tien 10
elf 11
twaalf 12
dertien 13
veertien 14
vijftien 15
zestien 16
zeventien 17
achttien 18

negentien 19
twintig 20
een en twintig 21
twee en twintig 22
dertig 30
veertig 40
vijftig 50
zestig 60
zeventig 70
tachtig 80
negentig 90
honderd 100
honderd een 101
twee honderd 200
twee honderd een 201
vijf honderd 500
vijf honderd vijf en twintig 525
duizend 1000

Days

maandag Monday
dinsdag Tuesday
woensdag Wednesday
donderdag Thursday
vrijdag Friday
zaterdag Saturday
zondag Sunday
gisteren yesterday
vandaag today
morgen tomorrow
morgenochtend tomorrow morning
jaar year
maand month

Flemish specialities

hutsepot a winter-warmer consisting of various bits of beef and pork (often including pigs' trotters and ears) casseroled with turnips, celery, leeks and parsnips.
konijn met pruimen rabbit with prunes.
paling in 't groen eel braised in a green (usually spinach) sauce with herbs.
stoemp mashed potato mixed with vegetable and/or meat purée.
stoofvlees cubes of beef marinated in beer and cooked with herbs and onions.
stoverij stewed beef and offal (especially liver and kidneys), slowly tenderized in dark beer and served with a slice of bread covered in mustard.
waterzooi a delicious, filling soup-cum-stew, made with either chicken (*van kip*) or fish (*van riviervis*).

week week
dag day

Months

januari January
februari February
maart March
april April
mei May
juni June
juli July
augustus August
september September
oktober October
november November
december December

Time

uur hour
minuut minute
Hoe laat is het? What time is it?
Het is... It's...
drie uur 3.00
vijf over drie 3.05
tien over drie 3.10
kwart over drie 3.15
tien voor half vier 3.20
vijf voor half vier 3.25
half vier 3.30
vijf over half vier 3.35
tien over half vier 3.40
kwart voor vier 3.45
tien voor vier 3.50
vijf voor vier 3.55
acht uur 's ochtends 8am
een uur 's middags 1pm
acht uur 's avonds 8pm
een uur 's nachts 1am

Food and drink terms

Basic terms and ingredients

belegd filled or topped, as in **belegde**
broodjes (bread rolls topped with cheese, etc)
boter butter
boterham/broodje sandwich/roll
brood bread
dranken drinks
eieren eggs
gerst barley

groenten vegetables
Hollandse saus hollandaise sauce
honing honey
hoofdgerechten main courses
kaas cheese
koud cold
nagerechten desserts
peper pepper
pindakaas peanut butter
sla/salade salad
smeerkaas cheese spread
stokbrood french bread
suiker sugar
vis fish
vlees meat
voorgerechten starters/hors d'oeuvres
vruchten fruit
warm hot
zout salt

Cooking methods

doorbakken well-done
half doorbakken medium well-done
gebakken fried or baked
gebraden roast
gegrild grilled
gekookt boiled
geraspt grated
gerookt smoked
gestoofd stewed
rood rare

Starters and snacks

erwtensoep/snert thick pea soup with bacon
or sausage
huzarensalade potato salad with pickles
koffietafel light midday meal of cold meats,
cheese, bread, and perhaps soup
patat/friet chips/french fries
soep soup
uitsmijter ham or cheese with eggs on bread

Meat and poultry

biefstuk (hollandse) steak
biefstuk (duitse) hamburger
eend duck
fricandeau roast pork
fricandel frankfurter-like sausage
gehakt minced meat
ham ham

kalfsvlees veal
kalkoen turkey
karbonade a chop
kip chicken
kroket spiced veal or beef in hash, coated in breadcrumbs
lamsvlees lamb
lever liver
ossenhaas tenderloin beef
rookvlees smoked beef
spek bacon
worst sausages

Fish and seafood

forel trout
garnalen prawns
haring herring
haringsalade herring salad
kabeljauw cod
makreel mackerel
mosselen mussels
oesters oysters
paling eel
schelvis haddock
schol plaice
tong sole
zalm salmon
zeeduivel monkfish

Vegetables

aardappelen potatoes
bloemkool cauliflower
bonen beans
champignons mushrooms
erwten peas
hutspot mashed potatoes and carrots
knoflook garlic
komkommer cucumber
prei leek
rijst rice
sla salad, lettuce
stampot andijvie mashed potato and endive
stampot boerenkool mashed potato and cabbage
uien onions
wortelen carrots
zuurkool sauerkraut

Sweets and desserts

appelgebak apple tart or cake

gebak pastry
ijs ice cream
koekjes biscuits
pannenkoeken pancakes
pepernoten ginger nuts
poffertjes small pancakes, fritters
(slag)room (whipped) cream
speculaas spice and cinnamon-flavoured biscuit
stroopwafels waffles
vla custard

Fruits

aardbei strawberry
amandel almond
appel apple
appelmoes apple purée
citroen lemon
druiven grape
framboos raspberry
kers cherry
peer pear
perzik peach
pruim plum/prune

Drinks

anijsmelk aniseed-flavoured warm milk
appelsap apple juice
bessenjenever blackcurrant gin
chocomel chocolate milk
citroenjenever lemon gin
droog dry
frisdranken soft drinks
jenever a Dutch/Belgian gin
karnemelk buttermilk
koffie coffee
koffie verkeerd coffee with warm milk
kopstoot beer with a **jenever** chaser
melk milk
met ijs with ice
met slagroom with whipped cream
pils beer
proost! cheers!
sinaasappelsap orange juice
thee tea
tomatensap tomato juice
vruchtensap fruit juice
wijn wine
(wit/rood/rosé) (white/red/rosé)
vieux Dutch brandy
zoet sweet

Glossary

Dutch terms

Abdij Abbey

Begijnhof Convent occupied by beguines (*begijns*), i.e. members of a sisterhood living as nuns but without vows, retaining the right of return to the secular world.

Beiaard Carillon (i.e. a set of tuned church bells, either operated by an automatic mechanism or played by a keyboard)

BG (Begane grond) Ground floor ("basement" is K for kelder)

Belfort Belfry

Beurs Stock exchange

Botermarkt Butter market

Brug Bridge

Burgher Member of the upper or mercantile classes of a town, usually with certain civic powers

Geen toegang No entry

Gemeente Municipal, as in Gemeentehuis (town hall)

Gerechtshof Law Courts

Gesloten Closed

Gevel Gable: decoration on narrow-fronted canal houses

Gilde Guild

Gracht Canal

Groentenmarkt Vegetable market

(Grote) markt Central town square and the heart of most north Belgian communities, normally still the site of weekly markets

Hal Hall

Hof Courtyard

Huis House

Ingang Entrance

Jeugdherberg Youth hostel

Kaai Quay or wharf

Kapel Chapel

Kasteel Castle

Kerk Church; eg Grote Kerk – the principal church of the town

Koning King

Koningin Queen

Koninklijk Royal

Korenmarkt Corn market

Kunst Art

Lakenhal Cloth hall: the building in medieval weaving towns where cloth would be weighed, graded and sold

Let Op! Attention!

Luchthaven Airport

Molen Windmill

Noord North

Ommegang Procession

Onze Lieve Vrouwekerk or OLV Church of Our Lady

Oost East

Paleis Palace

Plaats/Plein A square or open space

Polder An area of land reclaimed from the sea

Poort Gate

Postbus Post box

Raadhuis Town hall

Rijk State

Schatkamer Treasury

Schepenzaal Alderman's Hall

Schone kunsten Fine arts

Schouwburg Theatre

Sierkunst Decorative arts

Spoor Track (as in railway) – trains arrive and depart on track (as distinct from platform) numbers

Stadhuis town hall

Stedelijk Civic, municipal

Steeg Alley

Steen Stone

Stichting Institute or foundation

Straat Street

Toegang Entrance

Toren Tower

Tuin Garden

Uitgang Exit

VA (Vanaf) "from"

Vleeshuis Meat market

Volkskunde Folklore

Weg Way

West West

Zuid South

SMALL PRINT

Publishing Information
First edition 2018

Distribution

UK, Ireland and Europe
Apa Publications (UK) Ltd; sales@roughguides.com
United States and Canada
Ingram Publisher Services; ips@ingramcontent.com
Australia and New Zealand
Woodslane; info@woodslane.com.au
Southeast Asia
Apa Publications (SN) Pte; sales@roughguides.com
Worldwide
Apa Publications (UK) Ltd; sales@roughguides.com
Special Sales, Content Licensing and CoPublishing
Rough Guides can be purchased in bulk quantities at discounted prices. We can
create special editions, personalised jackets and corporate imprints tailored to
your needs. sales@roughguides.com.
roughguides.com
Printed in China by RR Donnelley Asia Printing Solutions Limited

A catalogue record for this book is available from the British Library
The publishers and authors have done their best to ensure the accuracy
and currency of all the information in **Pocket Rough Guide Bruges &
Ghent**, however, they can accept no responsibility for any loss, injury, or
inconvenience sustained by any traveller as a result of information or advice
contained in the guide.

Rough Guide Credits

Editor: Ros Walford
Cartography: Katie Bennett
Managing editor: Rachel Lawrence
Picture editor: Michelle Bhatia
Cover photo research: Sarah Stewart-
Richardson

Photographer: Anthony Cassidy / Jean
Christophe Godet
Original design: Richard Czapnik
Senior DTP coordinator: Dan May
Head of DTP and Pre-Press:
Rebeka Davies

Author
Phil Lee has been writing for Rough Guides for well over twenty years. His
other books in the series include Norway, Norfolk & Suffolk, Amsterdam,
Mallorca & Menorca and The Netherlands. He lives in Nottingham, where he
was born and raised.

Acknowledgements

Phil Lee would like to thank his editor, Ros Walford, for her thoroughgoing efficiency during the preparation of this book. Special thanks also to the superbly efficient Anita Rampall of Visit Flanders; Ann Plovie of Visit Bruges for her detailed assistance and suggestions; Lynn Meyvaert of Visit Gent for a string of tips and hints; Rob Haycocks of Eurostar for his kind help; Erwin van de Wiele, also of Visit Gent, for his hospitality and gastronomic tips; and the sound.

Help us update

We've gone to a lot of effort to ensure that the first edition of the **Pocket Rough Guide Bruges & Ghent** is accurate and up-to-date. However, things change – places get "discovered", opening hours are notoriously fickle, restaurants and rooms raise prices or lower standards. If you feel we've got it wrong or left something out, we'd like to know, and if you can remember the address, the price, the hours, the phone number, so much the better.

Please send your comments with the subject line "**Pocket Rough Guide Bruges & Ghent Update**" to mail@uk.roughguides.com. We'll credit all contributions and send a copy of the next edition (or any other Rough Guide if you prefer) for the very best emails.

Photo Credits

(Key: t-top; c-centre; b-bottom; l-left; r-right)

Alamy 23T, 23B, 25M, 25C, 25B, 26/27, 32, 41, 44, 58, 59, 63, 58, 80, 80, 81, 82, 87, 90, 103, 105, 106, 114, 115, 116, 117, 118, 120, 124, 136/137
Anthony De Meyere / Design Museum Gent 18B, 22B
Bistro Pro Deo 86
Cel Fotografie (Jan Termont) / Stad Brugge 24B, 49
City Damme / Jan Darthet 93
Diksmuids Boterhuis 33
Dirk Pauwels 15C
EKKOW / The Chocolate Line 16T
Galerie St-John, Ghent 112
Getty Images 2MC, 14B, 19T, 69, 110, 11, 121, 125,
iStock 2BL, 12, 16B, 17T, 20C, 28 ,29, 31, 57
Jan D'Hondt / Toerisme Brugge 6, 21B, 46, 83

Jürgen de Witte – www. jurgendewitte.be 25T
Kantcentrum 15B, 79
Ken Scicluna / AWL 1
Leonardo 128/129
Piet De Kersgieter 127
Pomperlut 68
Rough Guides 35, 45, 84, 85
Sarah Bauwens; Musea Brugge 17B, 20B, 50, 51, 52, 53
Shutterstock 2T, 2B, 4, 5, 13T, 13B, 14/15T, 18T, 19B, 20T, 21T, 21C, 22T, 22C, 23C, 24T, 24C, 30, 36, 37, 38, 39, 40, 42, 43, 47, 54, 56, 60, 61, 62, 64, 70, 71, 74, 75, 76, 78, 89, 91, 92, 94, 95, 98, 99,100, 101, 102, 104, 107, 109
Superstock.com 119
Sylvie Bonne 67
Tierenteyn 113
www.melvinkobe.com 126